# CHRISTIAN
# SCHOOL
# CURRICULUM:
# AN
# INTEGRATED
# APPROACH

Ronald P. Chadwick

BMH Books
P. O. Box 544
Winona Lake, Indiana 46590

# Dedication

To Dr. Roy W. Lowrie, Jr. who started me on this pursuit for integration, to Dr. Howard G. Hendricks who laid the solid educational foundation for integration, to my dear wife Sally for her challenge and ongoing encouragement in the quest for understanding integration and to our four sons Randall Scott, Stephen Michael, Robert Paul and Scott Michael who encouraged and helped me to learn how to practice integration.

My prayer is that as Christian parents and teachers we might more and more become men and women of God, who are men and women of the Book, who are men and women of integrity so that our sons and daughters and our students might demonstrate "character change that is Christ-like."

ISBN: 0-88469-228-0
COPYRIGHT 1990
BMH BOOKS
WINONA LAKE, INDIANA 46590


PRINTED IN USA


COVER DESIGN BY TERRY JULIEN

# Table of Contents

# Foreword

One of the greatest needs of the Christian school ministry is a practical approach to biblical integration. In his book, *Teaching and Learning*, Dr. Chadwick introduced one method by which this can be achieved. Now he takes the process he outlined in that book and makes practical application of it to a subject field—Social Studies.

This book can be extremely helpful to a teacher in any subject area at any grade level. The approach and process of integration uses the same principles regardless of the subject field. The concepts in this book will produce more effective teachers with the ability to integrate subject matter.

True biblical integration takes place in real life situations. That is, the teacher must understand and be committed to both the concept from the Bible and the concept from the subject field. Then the teacher must integrate the two concepts through his/her own practical experience. Truth in any subject field must be viewed from a biblical vantage point—not merely philosophically, but practically. This book will help any teacher make the practical application of integration in his/her planning and teaching.

One of the problems with integration attempts in the past has been the feeling that every part of every lesson must have some quotation from Scripture or a specific biblical thought attached to it. This is not necessarily true. God has revealed Himself to us in three ways—His Word, His Son, and His creation. With an integrated approach all of His revelation is brought into proper relationship. All truth must be understood and interpreted with biblical truth in mind. There can be no disagreement between biblical revelation and natural revelation. Where there is disagreement, the biblical principles must be in control.

Integration sometimes seems difficult because we have been trained to view some subject areas purely from a secular vantage point. However, if all truth is God's truth, then there cannot actually be disagreement between the truth of His Word and the truth of His creation.

The approach to integration outlined in this book does not pretend to be the only approach to the subject. However, if the reader will practice the concepts presented here, he/she will discover overriding integrated principles which can assist in the process of teaching from a biblical perspective.

Our goal as Christian educators is to train our students so they naturally begin to view all of truth as God's truth. It should be our goal to see our students thinking from a biblical perspective about all of life and all of learning. I commend this book to you for your personal and spiritual growth as well as your practical academic planning for true biblical integration.

Dr. James Braley

# Preface

My direct involvement with the study of integration began in 1972 with a workshop at the National Institute for Christian School Adminstrators entitled *Integration -- The Missing Ingredient.* From 1972 until 1977 there was further study and discussion regarding the subject of integration but as yet little was done specifically to demonstrate how integration could be done with a particular subject. It was decided to continue the study and discussion but to move into action and endeavor to apply the models developed to a specific subject area, namely Social Studies.

We called ourselves "The Task Force on Integration," and through the arrangements of Dr. Mel Carter we met in Dallas, Texas, at the First Baptist Academy. Dr. Carter and Dr. Warren Benson joined Mrs. Nancy Newton and myself to develop the basic structure for the project. Then Nancy Newton and I worked together hammering out the basic format and approach to the process of integration.

Why such an effort? To my knowledge never before has anyone endeavored to take a specific subject area and concept by concept, grade by grade, in a scope and sequence fashion demonstrate the capability of true integration. It was also believed that most Christian school teachers were already convinced of the *need* of integrating, but the problem was a practical one in that many simply did not know *how* and had nowhere to turn for a model to teach them the *process.*

Who participated in the project? In addition to those already mentioned ir the initiation of this particular project, we were also assisted by teachers fror. kindergarten through grade six at the following five Christian schools:

Norfolk Christian Schools, Norfolk, VA
Delaware County Christian Schools, Newton Square, PA
Scottsdale Christian Academy, Scottsdale, AZ
The Christian Academy, Brookhaven, PA
First Baptist Academy, Dallas, TX

The entire section dealing with the specific content or concepts to be taught K-6 are the contribution of Christian school teachers who are dealing with the subject matter regularly in the classroom. We felt that we needed to get firsthand input from people who were actually doing the teaching of the content and we discovered that there was a willingness on the part of Christian school teachers to share the information and the insights they had gained.

How has the project been developed? Utilizing the mastery objectives, scope and sequence chart from the Dallas Independent School District, Dallas, Texas, we have endeavored to apply the theory that has been presented in my book, *Teaching and Learning: An Integrated Approach to Christian Education* which is published by Fleming H. Revell Company. We have taken each concept (C.D. -- concept from the discipline) grade by grade covering the seven aspects of the social studies curriculum structure and have given a related biblical concept (B.C.) to demonstrate correlation; then have given an integrated statement which we call the biblically integrated concept (B.I.C.) The approach has been to integrate concept with concept which is the approach that we believe must be taken. This is the academic or theoretical aspects of integration. Following the biblical support or rationale for the biblical concept as well as the B.I.C. In some cases there is also an attempt to give suggestions for the life integrated aspects of the process of integration. This is the practical application step in integration. Often when integration is not possible theoretically concept with concept, integration is capable practically at the real life level.

So what! Certainly this is not the last word on the subject of integration, but it does take the theory and apply it specifically to a given subject area which we feel is a first and a must. We are sure that there is much room for improvement, but now the teacher at least at the K-6 level, if not at other levels as well, has a model or pattern to follow in pursuing further the subject of integration.

It has been my dream to develop integrated curriculum guides for every subject at every grade level, and then from the specific integrated curriculum guides to begin to develop quality integrated textbook material for use by the teachers in the classroom. The problem presently facing us is that the materials produced for us in the Christian schools are simply secular textbooks that have been "dry cleaned" or some materials written from a Christian perspective which lack a truly integrated approach. Some additional materials emphasize correlation and do make it easier for the teacher to engage in the process of integration. But very few of the materials available for the Christian school teacher truly demonstrate the integrated approach even though they are often called "integrated". This is an indication of how much remains to be done in the area of integration.

Hopefully, with truly integrated curriculum guides available, the classroom teacher who has the background and expertise in a particular subject area will be able to assist publishers and other Christian schools in the development of a series of truly integrated textbooks for use in Christian schools at every grade level, from kindergarten through college. With this as our prayer we trust that these materials will be able to assist teachers not only in integrating truth with truth, but ultimately in integrate truth with life and to produce the ultimate objective in Christian school education which is character change that is Christlike. "Unto the measure of the stature of the fullness of Christ" (Eph. 4:13).

Chapter 1

# Christian Education —
# An Integrated Approach*

Charles Shultz in a Peanuts cartoon pictures Snoopy out for some jogging and in the course of the running an interesting conversation takes place. "Just because I'm the right foot why do I have to do all the work?" The left foot responds, "What do you mean? I am the one who does all the cornering!" "Without us legs you feet would be nowhere . . ." "How can we concentrate with you guys talking all of the time?" "Oh sure, it's those stupid brains bragging again . . . They take credit for everything . . . Have you ever thought about why we are doing this?" "Just to keep the heart in shape!" Now the heart responds, "Just remember boys, if I go you all go!" Now both the left and the right feet respond, "That's scary!" "Shut up and keep running!"

Just as keeping the heart strong is crucial to maintaining good physical health, so it is just as crucial that we keep the heart in shape educationally in order for us to function effectively in the area of Christian education. But what is the heart of Christian education and what initially is the key ingredient? The heart of Christian education is our educational philosophy solidly based in and firmly built upon the truth of the Word of God. God has supernaturally revealed Himself to man through the revelation that is contained in the written Word. God has communicated divine truth to mankind, apart from which any pursuit of truth would become idle speculation and would have no validity in terms of divine eternal truth.

* Most of chapter 1 comes from chapter 8, *Christian School Education* written by the author and published in the volume edited by Kenneth O. Gangel, *Toward a Harmony of Faith and Learning* published by William Tyndale College Press, 1982. This chapter actually is a synopsis of Dr. Chadwick's first book, *Teach and Learning*.

## Presuppositions

The Christian educator accepts the principle of the priority of revelation to reason and thus accepts the fact that the Word of God is the final test of all truth. When men refuse to yield to the authority of Scripture, they are faced with the option of complete trust in the ability of human reason, but because of the fallible and finite nature of man, human reason can never be considered as a sufficient and independent criterion. When the infinite, infallible God has spoken on a subject there is nothing left for man to say. The first basic assumption, therefore, for the Christian educator is that the Bible, verbally inspired and inerrant in its entirety, is the final authority in all areas of Christian education. Recognizing that the Word of God is "alive and powerful and sharper than any two-edged sword," when we are reading the Bible it is not what God would say if He *were* here, but what God is saying because He *is* here.

The second major assumption for the Christian educator is that all truth is God's truth. Although there usually exists a dualistic concept of sacred and secular truth, it is assumed here that all truth is from the hand of God and is intended for man's use. God is the source, the *Quelle* of all truth that ever was, or is, or yet will be. A distinction still must be observed between revealed truth as declared by God and mundane truth as discovered by man, for man's relationship to his Creator is dependent upon the revelation of God in the Scriptures and not the discovered truth of man. However, assuming that all truth is the product of the mind of God, it must be subject to and evaluated in the light of the absolute criterion for determining truth. This absolute has been given in the form of the written Word, God's written revelation of Himself to man.

## God's Program

*In heaven's name what on earth are we to be doing?* What is God's program for today? On the basis of the Great Commission passages as given to us in Matthew 28:16-20, Mark 16:15, Luke 24:45-48, Acts 1:8, and John 20:21 it is impossible to say that God's program is soul-winning *or* teaching *or* evangelism *or* edification. It appears on the basis of these passages that God's program for this age is clearly a coin that has two sides. The first side involves the thrust of preaching or proclaiming the gospel while the reverse side emphasizes the need for edification or being built up in the faith. The New Testament teaches us that the most important work of the church when it is gathered together is to teach, to edify, to build up the believers. The church in the New Testament was not primarily a center for evangelism, but was in fact a school. The tragedy, however, is that some today are only emphasizing one side of the coin. We must never lose sight of the fact that the most important work of the church within the community is to make a penetration with the message of the gospel so that those who are lost and without Jesus Christ may be able to make an intelligent response to the gospel. The most important work within the church is teaching—edification, while the most important work outside the church is preaching—evangelism.

In your going into all the world, proclaim the gospel. Give the birth message of salvation to those who need to be born into the family of God. But don't stop there. Give them the growth message. Teach them the "all things" that they need in order that they might become mature, reproducing disciples of the Lord Jesus Christ. The purpose of God in His program for this age can be summarized by the one imperative verb of the Great Commission as recorded in Matthew 28:19: "Make disciples" (disciplize).

Thus in summary the purpose of Christian education is to glorify God by serving the home and the church in their task of making disciples.

**Definition of Education**

What is education and how specifically do we define Christian education? Education is both the process of acquiring significant learning experiences as well as the product of a desired change of personality and behavior. While education may be classified as formal, informal, and even nonformal, the test of education is not how much the student knows, but what kind of individual the educational process produces. If no observable character change is evident in the person who is supposedly involved in the educational process, then certainly the educational effort may be said to be woefully lacking. To have genuine education, personal change and personality development (the product) are essential. This is achieved through the process of guided, graded experience, meaningfully involving the learner. Change is something that the learner must experience. He must grow and develop, and if he does not do so, all of the so-called educational process expended to aid him is a failure.

Today educators recognize that the goal of education is the integration of a personality within a world view. Thus it may be concluded that education is the complete development of a personality for complete living consistent with a world view.

Education is a guided, graded process and presupposes the three essential elements of a teacher, a learner, and an environment in which learning may successfully take place. This guided, graded, ongoing process must assist the student in making the learning experiences his own, enabling him to develop as a person who acquires what he needs to ultimately become an individual who is capable of achieving his full potential.

Nowhere is character or behaviorial change and vital personal development more essential than in Christian education. The learner must exhibit outwardly what has taken place inwardly. He must give living, demonstrable proof of the power and strength of this individual commitment. Apart from this the processes of his educational experiences have miserably failed and he certainly is a mysterious product and a sad substitute for the real commodity, the genuine

Christian. The tragedy is that so many have been able to verbalize their Christianity without ever being able to actualize it and put it to work in flesh and blood.

## Negative Description of Christian Education

Christian education "is not an alias for evangelism." *It must be recognized that Christian education in the context of the school is not primarily in the business of producing Christians.* Though it is true especially during the younger grades that many children are brought into vital relationships with Jesus Christ, the Christian school, and particularly the Christian college, is not the intellectual counterpart of the revival meeting. True Christian education can never take place until the student is indwelled by the One who "guides you into all truth" (John 15:13). Prior to this time the student is only receiving an education in a Christian atmosphere.

Furthermore, Christian education is not just having a faculty or student body composed of Christians. It is just as true, however, that apart from these two prerequisites Christian education cannot exist. These, however, are not a guarantee. When Robert Louis Stevenson was informed by his wife that the maid was a good church girl, he is alleged to have replied, "Then I would like some Christian broth." Just as a church girl could not make Christian broth, so the combination of a Christian teacher and pupil does not guarantee that the education is distinctively Christian. Even compulsory attendance at chapel services or other religious exercises does not produce Christian education.

The sponsorship of the school is not the deciding factor in whether the education is Christian. Many traditional Christian colleges controlled by denominational groups have long since forsaken the principles of Christian education. In some it is because there are men and women on the faculty who cannot fulfill the first qualification of being a Christian and in others it is because they are controlled by religious indifferentists. In such cases it would be easier to attempt Christian education with a Christian faculty in a state school than it would be on the campuses of these so-called Christian schools.

In addition to these criteria, the inclusion or exclusion of any course from the school curriculum does not guarantee Christian education. In other words, just because the Bible is taught in a school does not make the education Christian, nor does its absence as a separate course of study make the education secular. From this it can be seen that content or subject matter alone does not determine whether or not a school is engaged in education that is distinctively Christian.

## Positive Definition of Christian Education

A Christian philosophy of education emphasizing the theocentric view seeks to formulate a unified and coherent concept of God and His Word in the creation and nature of man. Thus, theistic philosophy becomes the central integrating core of Christian education. If such be the case, the educational process should develop the complete person of God, completely fitted for every good work for the glory of God and the good of mankind. The measure of this complete person will be the stature of Christ, who is the core and integrator of the totality of Christian education.

This process of education will produce individuals who are not only capable of functioning within society but also capable of functioning effectively within the body of Christ, "Unto the measure of the stature of the fullness of Christ" (Ephesians 4:13).

Christian education does not merely have an emphasis upon teaching concepts but rather upon communicating life principles. Because of this, it has as its goal "the perfecting of the saints unto the work of ministering, unto the building up of the body of Christ" (Ephesians 4:12), "that we may present every man perfect (complete) in Christ" (Colossians 1:28), "in order that (hina, Ephesians 4:14) we will in all things grow up into Him" (Ephesians 4:15NIV) and demonstrate Biblical wisdom (Colossians 1:9).

## Philosophy of Teaching-Learning

What is our distinctive philosophy of teaching-learning from a biblical perspective? Is the teacher's role primarily that of a disseminator of information or is it primarily the role of a facilitator of learning?

Educators generally are in agreement that teachers teach as they were taught. Scripture gives us some interesting insights along these lines in Luke 6:39-40 as well as in Matthew 10:24-25. The Luke 6 passage literally translated says, "Can one blind person guide another, shall they not both fall into the ditch? A disciple is not above his teacher, but everyone having been perfected will be as his teacher." The Scripture is saying to us that as the teacher is, so the student will become.

Are there any specific passages of Scripture that give a model for the teaching-learning process? Certainly Deuteronomy 6 puts the emphasis on teaching in such a way that people might be able to learn by observation. Moses outlines the steps involved in ultimately producing the desired result: The Word of God becomes the controlling factor in the actions, attitudes, private and public life of the individual. Matthew 28 and the words of our Lord emphasize teaching that should be done in such a way that the people might be able to observe the teachings that they have come to know. Probably 1 Thessalonians chapter 1 is one of the most complete passages dealing with the subject of the model teacher and model teaching. It provides some valuable insights. Paul begins in verse 2 by emphasizing the preparation necessary as he stresses making mention of them unceasingly in His prayers. He picks it up then in verse 5 and emphasizes that the gospel came "not to you in Word only, but even in power, and in the Holy Spirit, and in much assurance; as you know what manner of men we were among you for your sake." Then Paul says that they became followers, literally imitators, of Him and as a result, even of the Lord welcoming the Word in much affliction with joy of the Holy Spirit. The result of this is seen in verses 7 and 8 where he says that they became an "ensample," literally a model or pattern, to all of the ones believing in Macedonia or Achaia, "but also in every place your faith to God is spread abroad so that we need not to speak anything." Apparently, Paul is emphasizing that we must be concerned not only with the content that is being taught, but even how it is being taught, as well as the life of the individual who is actually doing the teaching.

The apostle Paul not only in 1 Thessalonians chapter 1, but also in Colossians chapter 1 verses 9 and 10, stresses that true learning begins with the facts about God and ends with an increased knowledge of God, but the real goal is to produce godliness. True learning begins with the information about God's plan and purpose and ends with the knowledge of His person, but again the ultimate goal is to produce a "perfect" man. The Bible communicates to us that learning just for the sake of learning, to amass knowledge, is not acceptable. The Bible says that true learning is for living. This is even seen in Hebrews 5:11-14 where the writer says: "Concerning whom we have much to say and hard to interpret since you have become dull in your hearings. For indeed because of the time you ought to be teachers you have need that someone teach you again the rudiments of the beginnings of the oracles of God and you have become as those having need of milk and not of solid food. For everyone partaking of milk is without experience of the Word of righteousness for he is an infant" (author's translation). Now the King James translation of verse 14 says that they were unskillful in the Word of righteousness and this is often interpreted to mean that the individual did not have the ability to properly understand, interpret, and teach the Word. Even though this may be involved, the true meaning of unskillful is that they were lacking experience in relationship to the Word of righteousness. In other words, they knew the truth but they were not experiencing it in their daily life and true teaching-learning in Christian education requires life application.

**Philosophy of Curriculum**

In the philosophy of curriculum according to the traditional approach to education as viewed in Herbart, the outer factors of the pupil are emphasized and it becomes teacher-centered. In progressive education as illustrated in the teachings of John Dewey, the inner factors are stressed with the result that the education becomes pupil-centered. For years Christians have been content to subscribe to whatever educational ideas were prevalent at the time, all the way from Herbart and traditionalism to Dewey and progressivism. However, since it is true that Christian education is distinctive, then it is not legitimate to have the same integrating factor in a distinctive Christian philosophy of education as would be found in a manmade system.

The word *curriculum* is derived from the Latin, *currere*, which means "to run," and in ancient Rome referred to "running on a race course." Traditionally the course or curriculum was considered the body of content that the student covered in his educational progress. More recently the term connotes the activities of the student as he is engaged in various experiences which involve content.[3]

However, the question of the center, the integrating force, becomes crucial in structuring curriculum. As Christians we must see that an authoritative content and personal experience are paramount to the total development of the personality within the framework of a Christian theistic world view.

Can Christians accomplish their aims and objectives in a curriculum that is man-centered? Some have proposed that only a God-centered curriculum can be Christian, and this is absolutely correct, for without God an atheistic world view is all that remains. However, the only revelation of God Himself and His Son which provides for restoration and fellowship between Creator and creature is the written Word of God, and He never meant that the written Word should be separated from the living Word. Christian education must be a balance of both content and experience, truth and life. Apart from the written Word (content), the living Word (experience) can never be known. Thus, the concepts of a God-centered and Bible-centered approach are drawn together as intended by God in the clearer concept of a Word-centered approach. No other center can compare for its immutability, vitality, and power. Thus in the approach of a concept-competence curriculum, from a Christian perspective, there is an attempt to integrate the student's cognitive development with the development of his total personality in relation to a thoroughly biblical world and life view for the purpose of producing character change that demonstrates maturity in Jesus Christ. This approach to curriculum is solidly based in and dependent upon God's revelation, but not without reasonably and rationally tying it to reality.

## Integration[4]

Historically, the word *Christian* has always referred to a world view based upon the Bible. To attempt Christian education by adding a Christian frosting to the cake of a manmade and man-centered philosophy is neither consistent with Christianity nor is it distinctive. All four of the basic areas of curricular content (1) abstract science, (2) social science, (3) physical science and (4) fine arts, must be interpreted and integrated within the recognized world view; therefore, for a Christian it must be a Christian theistic world view. What then is integration? Probably much of what has been attempted in the past in the area of integration in Christian education has been much closer to correlation. According to Webster, to correlate means to "have a common relation." To correlate is to "show a causal relationship to two things" or it directly implies that two things are complementary to each other, such as husband and wife. Therefore, to take two concepts that are common to each other and correlate them would simply be to show their common relationship. On the other hand, to integrate these concepts would be to unite them together into a single larger, expanded unit. Integration is the bringing together of parts into a whole, and so with integration in Christian education it is the living union not only of concepts with concepts, of truth with truth, but it is the living union of the subject matter in the life not only of the teachers but the administration as well as the students. The eternal, infinite pattern of God's written truth must be woven together with all of truth and all of life.

Because secular education today has deliberately departed from God and His Word, it will continue to search, ever learning and yet not able to come to a knowledge of the truth. Having turned its back upon God and His Word, secular education is powerless to put together its eternal meaning. There is no integrating factor that is consistent throughout the entire system. Christian education, however, is quite different. With all its inadequacy, failures, and difficulties, it has a firm foundation. Christian education does not need to keep looking for the integrating factor—it already has its integrating factor.

Many Christian schools today are Christian in name only and fail to reflect a thoroughgoing Christian center of education. Every realm of knowledge, every aspect of life, and every fact of the universe finds its place and meaning within the scope of Christianity. As Dr. Edwin Rian has said, "The present tendency in education to add religion to the courses of study is comparable to attaching a garage to a home. What the building of knowledge needs is not a new garage but a new foundation. . . ." The Word of God or a Christian theistic world view provides this foundation and the written Word and the living Word, the Lord Jesus Christ, provide for us in education the core or center or integrating factor that is so crucial.[5]

The apostle John in John 1:14 states, "The Word became flesh and dwelt among us and we beheld him. . . ." Essentially what John was saying is that we saw Him, we touched Him and we beheld His glory. We saw Him operate. We saw Him reflect the realities of what He spoke, and we saw that there was

## THREE ASPECTS OF INTEGRATION

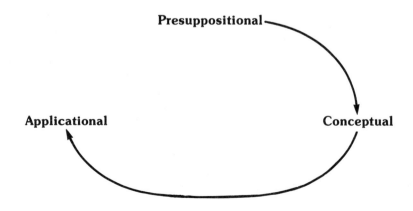

(See Chapter 6, especially page 65)

consistency not only in the words He spoke but in the life He lived. What our students need to see so desperately today is a clear, observable model of the reality of Jesus Christ, and a communication both by words and by life that it is absolutely feasible to live a life of faith. This is not only the integration of truth but Truth/truth with life. When this is achieved then maturity in Christ can be developed and the ultimate goal of Christian education is accomplished.

1. See chapter 5 for a more complete discussion of a biblical philosophy of teaching-learning.
2. See chapter 4 for a more complete discussion of curriculum.
3. Lois E. LeBar, *Education That Is Christian* (Old Tappen, N.J.: Fleming H. Revell Co., revised 1981), p. 203.
4. See chapter 3 for a more complete discussion of integration.
5. Edwin H. Rian, *Chirstianity and American Education* (San Antonio: Naylor Co., 1949), p. 236.

Chapter 2

# The Missing Teacher Ingredient—
# Integrity*

What is the one most essential quality or characteristic that could become the key ingredient or secret formula for success?

Possibilities like faith, hope or love are often suggested and are indeed important. Hebrews 11:6 says that without faith it is impossible to please God. Faith certainly is the bottom line, for without faith the person could not even be called a child of God. Yet, as important as faith is as a foundation, it is not the missing ingredient in teacher success.

First Corinthians 13:13 says, "And now abideth faith, hope and love, these three, but the greatest of these is love." But even as important as love is, is it the missing ingredient today?

Harold Blake Walker, in his syndicated column in the *Chicago Tribune Magazine*, July 20, 1980, gives this insight:

> Years ago after the close of World War II, I read an article describing the fall of France. One sentence in it has remained in my mind: "France did not fall when the Germans came. France fell 10 years earlier when one word went out of the French vocabulary and that word was 'integrity.' "
>
> Whether the article accurately portrayed the state of ethical failure of France before the war is a matter of debate, but there can be no debate over the fact that when integrity goes out of a nation's vocabulary, that nation is in the process of disintegration. It is trust in the men and the institutions of society that is the foundation of order. Where integrity is lacking, mutual confidence and trust erodes.
>
> There are unfortunate signs that integrity is on the wane in our society: bribery, misuse of campaign funds, corrupting federal and state govern-

ments, colleges and universities altering academic grades to allow athletes to play football or basketball, insurance companies being cheated through false claims, shoplifting becoming commonplace; it is obvious that "integrity" is slipping from our national vocabulary.

When General William Dean was captured by the North Koreans, he was permitted to write one letter home. He wrote to his son and said, "Bill, remember that integrity is the most important thing of all. Let it always be your aim." The writer of Proverbs 20:7 puts his finger on the key word, "The righteous man walks [not in his faith, not in his hope and not in his love; but the righteous man walks] in his integrity: blessed, happy, or fortunate are his children after him" (Berkeley).

This is also the key word as far as Job was concerned. After Job began to suffer, Job's wife said to him, "Do you still hold fast to your integrity?" (Job 2:3). And Job answers, "Till I die I will not remove mine integrity!" (Job 27:5), and ". . . that God may know mine integrity" (Job 31:6). Job is saying that even if he loses everything, including life itself, the one thing that he wants God to always remember him for is his integrity.

What is integrity? It is interesting that the word integrity comes from the same root word from which we get our word integer. Now in the field of mathematics an integer is a whole number. Integrity is wholeness. Many times we demonstrate certain qualities at certain times or in certain areas or even on certain days, but we do not do it consistently in the totality or in the whole of our life.

Negatively an integer is a number that has not yet been divided into fractions. A man or a woman of integrity is not fractionalized. Our Lord says, "The house that is divided against itself cannot stand" (Mark 3:25). James says, "A double minded man is unstable in all his ways" (James 1:8).

What is the missing ingredient that, if we could put it back into our homes, our churches and our schools, would provide the key to give us the wholeness and consistency we need? It is *integrity*. The amazing thing about this is that the Bible not only gives us negative and positive examples of integrity but also a model for developing integrity.

The negative example begins in 1 Samuel 2:12. "Now the sons of Eli were sons of Belial; they knew not the Lord." In a twentieth century context, Eli was pastor of a church. He had two sons and neither of his sons were believers following the way of God. They were Satan worshippers involved in gross immorality. "Now Eli was very old and heard all that his sons did unto all Israel; and how they lay with the women that assembled at the door of the tabernacle of the congregation" (1 Samuel 2:22). These sons were carrying on open prostitution right on the doorsteps of the church, right out in the parking lot. He "heard all that his sons did . . . and how they lay with the women that assembled at the door of the tabernacle of the congregation." And Eli said unto his two sons, "Why do ye such things? For I hear of your evil dealings by all this people. Nay, my sons; for it is no good report that I hear." That's the understatement of the hour! "It's no good report that I hear." In this situation, the law was quite clear and Eli was not ignorant of the law. He knew his responsibility. Apart from the divine intervention of the grace of God, Eli had only one option; to take his two sons, Hophni and Phinehas, and have them stoned to death. Though the law was clear and Eli knew exactly what to do, all he said was, "Nay, my sons, it is no good report that I hear." Then he went on to say, "Why, you're making the Lord's people to transgress." Didn't Eli realize that by the way he handled the situation he also caused the Lord's people to transgress? He was the leader. He was not only the father, but also the priest.

Well, the story goes on. In 1 Samuel 2:34, God intervenes: "And this shall be a sign unto thee, that shall come upon thy two sons, Hophni and Phinehas: in one day they shall die, both of them." God says, "All right, Eli, if you're not willing to take the situation in hand, then I'm going to have to deal with it. I cannot allow this to continue. That's that!" And Hophni and Phinehas are gone. They die, both of them in the same day. But even that is not the end of the story. We get an additional glimpse at God's attitude toward this whole situation in 1 Samuel 3:13. "For I have told him that I will judge his house forever." According to the law, the sin of one generation could affect how many generations? Exodus 20 says, "unto the third and the fourth generation." But here it says, I have told him that I will judge his house *forever.*" Why the severity of the judgment? Well, the passage is clear. "For the iniquity which he knoweth"—he knew very well what was going on. Eli's house was going to be judged forever for the iniquity which he knew, because his sons made themselves vile, because of their involvement concerning their sexual sins, and it says, "He restrained them not!" God was not dealing with Eli on the basis of what he did not know but what he did know. For us today our prayer should be, "Lord, help us to have the courage to face and deal with everything we do know, but help us not to worry about the things we don't know. Lest you think God's judgment harsh, that Eli *could not* restrain the evil activity of his sons, let's look at the Dutch translation of this particular verse. It says, " and he did not even give them a sour look." That is really the idea from the Hebrew. "He did not even give them a moment of time to scowl at them, to somehow convey to them that, what they were doing was wrong; stop it!" Eli did not give them a moment of his time until it was too late. God says, "Eli, I am going to judge you; and I am going to judge your house forever, because you knew what was going on and you knew what your responsibility was. I am going to judge you, and I am going to judge your household; and it is going to be forever."

The amazing thing is that Eli was apparently not having severe problems in terms of his spiritual ministry and responsibilities with the people, even though he had this terrible problem in his home.

You want to build a strong church? Build strong homes. You want to build a strong Christian school? Then build strong homes. Build strong family units.

If we could put integrity back into our Christian homes and then integrity into our churches and schools, then we would be able to deal with the problems we face today.

Now let us look at a positive example. At first I thought that David, along with Eli and Samuel, were simply negative illustrations. Upon closer examination I discovered that David is actually a positive example of integrity. First Kings 9:4 says, "And if thou wilt walk before me, as David thy father walked, in integrity of heart, and in uprightness, to do according to all that I have commanded thee, and will keep my statutes and my judgments: then I will establish the throne of thy kingdom upon Israel forever, as I promised to David thy father, saying, there shall not fail thee a man upon the throne of Israel." Thus 1 Kings 9:4 clearly states that God calls David a man of integrity.

But the question of course is, how can David, after his sin with Bathsheba, be classified as a man of integrity? The answer is found in 2 Samuel 12:1-13. There Nathan gives a parable to David. It is a story of a rich man who had many flocks and herds and a poor man who had nothing except one little ewe lamb. When a stranger came to visit the rich man, instead of taking an animal from his own herds and flocks, he took the ewe lamb from the poor man and prepared it for a great feast for the stranger who had come to visit him. When David heard the story, his anger was greatly kindled against the man, and he insisted that the man should restore the lamb fourfold because he had done this thing and had shown no pity. At that point, Nathan said to David, "Thou art the man" (2 Samuel 12:7). In this situation, Nathan lovingly nailed David to the wall. But what is David's response? In verse 7 the finger was put on David. Then in verse 13 he responded and said to Nathan, "I have sinned against the Lord." Immediately Nathan said to David, "The Lord also hath put away thy sins; thou shalt not die."

Apparently, as the result of David's confession, he was not only forgiven, but there was actually cleansing. In addition, it seems apparent that there was even a demonstration of the divine intervention of the grace of God; for, according to the law, David should have been killed because of his sin with Bathsheba. But Nathan specifically said that David would not die.

The issue that needs to be understood from the story of David is not whether we will or will not sin. John says, "These things write I to you that you sin not at all. But if any man sin—and I know you will, we have an advocate with the Father, Jesus Christ the righteous" (1 John 2:1). Scripture makes it very clear that we are all sinners and that we will sin. The issue is when we become aware of our sins, how will we respond? In David's case his integrity was restored, because as soon as he was confronted with his sin he confessed. The result was that the lost integrity was regained.

Apparently, the six hardest words in the English language, "I am wrong, I am sorry," are necessary and appropriate for teachers, as well as parents, when they are really wrong. Never do adults have the right to be wrong when they are working with children or young people; and in order for integrity to be maintained or restored, the situation must be honestly faced, and confessed. What we desperately need in our homes, our churches, Christian schools, colleges, and seminaries are people who know the Word and who are living by it in the totality of their lives. Our students and children will have a much better chance of becoming Godly men and women of integrity if we as Christian parents and leaders demonstrate a model of integrity. May God enable us to demonstrate the missing ingredient. "The righteous man walks in his integrity. Blessed (happy or fortunate) are his children after him" (Proverbs 20:7). Now let's look at a positive model for developing integrity.

> Now these are the commandments, the statutes, and the judgments, which the Lord your God commanded to teach you, that ye might do them in the land whither ye go to possess it:
> That thou mightest fear the Lord thy God, to keep all His statutes and His commandments, which I command thee, thou, and thy son, and thy son's son, all the days of thy life; and that thy days may be prolonged.
> Hear therefore, O Israel, and observe to do it; that it may be well with thee, and that ye may increase mightily, as the Lord God of thy fathers hath promised thee, in the land that floweth with milk and honey.
> Hear, O Israel: The Lord our God is one Lord:
> And thou shalt love the Lord thy God with all thine heart, and with all thy soul, and with all thy might.
> And these words, which I command thee this day, shall be in [upon] thine heart:
> And thou shalt teach them diligently unto thy children, and shalt talk of them when thou sittest in thine house, and when thou walkest by the way, and when thou liest down, and when thou risest up.
> And thou shalt bind them for a sign upon thine hand, and they shall be as frontlets between thine eyes.
> And thou shalt write them upon the posts of thy house, and on thy gates.
> (Deuteronomy 6:1-9)

In this passage of Scripture Moses emphasizes the necessity for teaching children. It is important to note that as far as Scripture is concerned, every command that relates to the nurturing and training of children has always been given to parents. None are addressed to the school or the church. You say, "Wait a minute. Are you trying to put down the Christian school or the church?" Not at all! You see, the Christian school and our churches have a responsibility to help us as parents with our children. God has given parents to children to nurture, train, and discipline them, and God has given the church to parents to nurture, train and discipline them. In these days God has raised up the Christian school to help Christian parents to be able to raise children so that they might become men and women of God but not to do it for us. But Moses, in Deuteronomy 6:1-3 says, "teach to observe to do!" He is saying, "Teach in such a way that your children will be able to observe in terms of the quality of their life."

The Bible says that learning is always for the purpose of living and this learning is always in relationship to life-relatedness. To equip us to be able to live better for the glory of our Lord. So Moses says, "Teach! Teach to observe! Teach to observe to do!" Then, in the latter part of verse three and verse four, Moses says, "Hear O Israel, the Lord our God is one Lord." If we could put that into a twentieth century context so that you and I could understand what Moses is talking about, he is simply saying to us that the starting point, the foundation upon which you and I have to build, is the Lord! And for us today, it is the Lord as He has revealed Himself to us in the Word of God! What Moses is pointing to here in Deuteronomy 6:4 is the absolute essentiality of the inspiration and the authority of the Word of God as the foundation upon which we have to build.

But Moses is not only talking about the importance of the inspiration and the authority of the Word of God as a foundation upon which you and I have to build; but, he is also talking about inspiration and the authority of the Word of God as a weight or a burden to exert pressure in our life. When he says, "And thou shalt love the Lord thy God with all thine heart, with all thy soul, and with all thy might and these words which I command you this shall be in [upon] thine heart," Moses speaks of God's Word as a weight or a burden. The implication is that the Word of God ought to exert pressure to guide, govern and control in the totality of our lives. Matthew 11:29-30 says, "Come unto me, all ye that labor and are heavy laden, and I will give you rest." Sometimes when we go through the rough winters in the north country, we think of rest as a chaise lounge on Miami Beach! Unfortunately, that is not what the Scripture says. Do you know how you and I get rest as far as God is concerned? We get rest when we are willing to stick our neck into the yoke which God has prepared for us to link ourselves up with Him. He says, "My yoke is easy and my burden is light." The Word of God, as a weight or a burden, is not to weigh us down or destroy us in terms of our effectiveness. The Word of God becomes a weight or a burden in the sense that it puts pressure on every area of our life. The Word has implications in every area to control and give direction and guidance. It's one thing to hold the Word of God in your hand. It's another thing to allow the Word of God to hold you and that's what Moses is stressing.

I remember well a few years ago when our youngest was still a baby. My wife was working feverishly to get supper ready. Scott was really fussy—he was hungry, tired, and cranky. Mom said to the oldest son, "Randy, take Scott and see if you can't keep him happy until I get supper finished." She had also told one of the other boys to get a garbage bag from the cupboard and put the garbage bag into the container. Everyone was doing what he was supposed to be doing. As Randy came around the corner into the kitchen with little Scott on his shoulder, he did not see his younger brother down on the floor with the garbage bag. He stumbled and tripped. Scott went flying out of his arms and into the cupboard. My wife let out a scream. I raced into the kitchen, picked up the baby and as I went past my wife, said, "Sweetheart, I'm on my way to the emergency room. Call the doctor." I was gone with Scott for over two hours. The doctor assured me his injury was not serious. When I came back, two of my sons met me at the front door. One of the boys said, "Dad, everything is all right." I asked if they had talked to the doctor. "No," they said, "the doctor didn't call. When you left the house, Mom did exactly as you told her to do. She called the doctor. Then, as soon as she finished talking, she gathered us together and we went into the living room and knelt down by the couch and began to pray. Dad, we prayed until we were sure everything was all right."

We build our life on the firm foundation and the banner over us is not just love, but the banner over us is the Word of God. The Word of God is the foundation upon which we build, but the Word of God is a weight or a burden to exert pressure in terms of guiding, governing and controlling in the totality of our lives.

It is interesting that Deuteronomy 6:7 talks about indoctrination. That word causes an automatic negative reaction. To some, indoctrination means brainwashing. They are not the same at all. Indoctrination is made up of the preposition "in" and the word "doctrine." What we are really talking about here is building into the lives of our children and our young people the basic truth or concepts that we hold to be essential. We are building into their lives the doctrinal truths that they need to know. It is not giving them all of the answers because we do not even know what all of the questions are. It is building the principles that will give them the ability to make decisions or judgments that are completely consistent with the Word of God. Deuteronomy 6:7 says, "And thou shalt teach them diligently unto thy children." This literally means "cutting deeply into their minds or their thought patterns." From the Christian perspective it is more than a matter of being exposed to various philosophies. It is a matter of saying, "Thus saith the Lord!" The truths or principles from God's Word have to be built into the lives of our children.

One of the ways that you and I make a tremendous impact on the lives of our children is by the way we live—by the model or pattern that we set before them. The tragedy is that most parents don't spend much time with their children. The average father spends thirty-two seconds a day with a child under one year of age. By the time the child reaches the fourth or fifth grade, the average father spends about fifteen minutes per week with the child. It is obvious that you and I are not going to be able to teach our children diligently on that basis. You say, "But my children are in a Christian school." I thank God for Christian school teachers and administrators and the impact they have had on the lives of our boys. The prayer life of one of my sons was revolutionized by a Christian school teacher. His whole attitude toward reading the

Bible and having a time alone with God was changed. My sons not only need to see this in the lives of their school teachers, but they need to see this in the lives of their parents. Here, the Word of God is talking not only about the formal kind of instruction but about informal instruction that we give to our children when we sit in our house, when we walk by the way, when we lie down, and when we rise up. There is a sense in which Moses is saying to us that Christian education is a twenty-four-hour job. That is the reason why, as a Christian parent, I want a pastor, Sunday school teacher, youth leader, Christian school administrator, and Christian school teachers on my team. I need their help to accomplish the job of building truths from God's Word into my children. So the emphasis here is not only on the Word of God as the foundation to guide, govern, and control in the totality of our lives, but it is also on indoctrinating our children with the basic principles from God's Word that will give them the ability to live the truth as Christians.

The Word of God doesn't stop there. God's Word says if you and I are building this into the lives of our children, the result will be integrity—integration. "And thou shalt bind them for a sign upon thine hand, and they shall be as frontlets between thine eyes, and thou shalt write them upon the posts of thy house, and on thy gates" (Deuteronomy 6:8-9). Moses is talking about the Word of God controlling all areas of our life—including our actions; "the hands" "Frontlets between your eyes"—our attitudes and thought life; "doorposts"— the private life of our home and family; and the "gate"—our public contacts.

What about the order Moses gives us? It appears from Scripture that attitudes come first, then actions. You know, "As a man thinks in his heart, so is he" (Proverbs 23:7). But Moses is saying to us, "The way to change your attitudes and thoughts is by changing your actions." Let me illustrate.

A couple comes to me with a marital problem—"We're going to get a divorce. We're not in love anymore."

"What do you mean, you're not in love anymore? Was there a time that you were in love?"

"Oh, yes, when we first were married, but not anymore."

Then I say, "What's different now as opposed to when you were in love?"

"Back then we used to do loving things for one another. I'd take her special places, get things for her, and do special things to show her how much I really loved her. But now that we've stopped loving each other, we've stopped doing special things."

They have it twisted around. The way you develop a loving attitude toward another person is by showing love. Is there someone in your family, school or church who "bugs" you? I faced this situation once. I knelt and said, "Lord, change my attitude about Brother So-and-So!" The problem was, when I got off my knees, nothing had changed! But that was when the Lord showed me that attitudes change by changing one's actions. Thus I began to pray, "Lord, help me to have the spiritual courage and intestinal fortitude to reach out and do something kind and loving for this brother." My attitude began to change. Eventually, we developed a warm friendship.

Moses teaches that the Word of God must control every area of our lives. The problem is the Word may be deposited in the mind, but not reach the heart to change actions and attitudes. We must be men and women made whole through God's Word transforming our lives. Not only in terms of our actions and our attitudes, but in the public and private areas of our lives as well. The person who allows the Word of God to control every area is truly a man or woman of integrity. A man or woman who demonstrates wholeness has the Word of God in control in every area of life. Often the problem is that the Word of God has been deposited in the mind, but it has not really gotten to the heart. Psalm 119:11 says, "Thy Word have I hid in my heart,"—not just my head. You can not have the Word of God in your heart until you first have it in your head. The tragedy is that you can memorize it and have it in your head and not have it affect you in the totality of your life. We must be men and women who can think Christianly and can live Christianly.

Often I will say to Christian school people that the ultimate objective in Christian education is character change that is Christ-like. That is a matter of allowing the truths of the Word of God and Jesus Christ to have impact in the totality of life. It can also be stated this way: The ultimate objective in Christian education is to develop the integrated Christian—a man or woman of God who is a man or woman of integrity.

Often I have said to my students, "My first concern for you is not that you become Christian educators. My first concern is that you become men and women of God who follow the Book." But I have found that I have had to add another phrase, "a man or woman of God who is a man or woman of the Book, who is also a man or woman of integrity."

Our boys and girls will have a much better chance of becoming men and women of God who are men and women of the Book who are men and women of integrity, if we as Christian parents and as Christian school leaders will demonstrate a model of integrity. May God enable us to develop this missing ingredient. "The righteous man walks in his integrity, blessed (happy or fortunate) are his children after him" (Proverbs 20:7).

Chapter 3

# The Missing Teaching Ingredient — Integration

## Introduction

There's an old adage in the real estate business that real estate valuation is dependent upon three things: location, Location, and LOCATION. I'd like to suggest a new adage for Christian education. Christian education valuation is dependent upon three things: integration, Integration, and INTEGRATION.

## What is Integration?

### What Integration Is Not!

Now that we have suggested a definition of Christian education in chapter 1, our next step is to answer the question, what is integration?

Much of Christian education in the past has been secular education with a chocolate coating of Christianity. The morning devotion, prayer or Bible reading was to exert a hallowed influence upon the work of the day. But even the addition of a Bible course to the regular curriculum is only adding religion to an essentially secular content.

The term *Christian* has always referred to a world view based on the Bible. Christian education cannot be based on a man-centered philosophy that is not consistent with Christianity. All curricular content in the elementary and secondary schools must be interpreted and integrated within the recognized world view, and therefore for a Christian it must be a Christian theistic world view!

**What Integration Is!**

What then is integration? Probably much of what has been attempted in the past in the area of integration in Christian education has been much closer to correlation than integration. According to Webster, to correlate means to "have a common relation." To correlate is to "show a causal relationship to two things" or directly implies that two things are complementary to each other, such as husband and wife. Therefore, to take two concepts that are common to each other and to *correlate* them would simply be to show their common relationship, while to *integrate* two concepts would be to unite them together into a single unit, which possibly is expanded as a result of the two being united.

A further difference between correlation and integration is this: if bringing the two concepts together really doesn't contribute to the ongoing of the subject, then it is correlation, while integration of the two concepts would promote the ongoing of the subject, demonstrating that all truth is God's truth. Integration is the bringing together of parts into a whole, and so integration in Christian education is the living union of not only concepts with concepts, of truth with TRUTH, but the living union of the subject matter with life—the eternal, infinite pattern of God's written Truth woven together with all truth and all of life.

The question of the center or the integrating force in education certainly is crucial. As Christians, we must see that an authoritative content and personal experience are paramount to the total development of the personality within the framework of the Christian theistic world-view. The only revelation of God Himself and His Son which provides for the restoration of fellowship between Creator and creature is the written Word of God, and He never meant that the written Word should be separated from the living Word. Apart from the written Word, the living Word can never be known. Thus the concept of a God-centered and Bible-centered approach to education are drawn together as intended by God Himself in the clearer concept of a Word-centered approach. No other integrating factor or core can match its immutability, vitality and power.

# Why Is Integration Essential?

Why is the subject of integration so essential? Though it is true that education is commonly divided into two categories, "secular" and religious," the Christian who has seriously thought this through cannot accept this dualistic approach to education, nor can he accept this dualistic approach to life.

### Biblical Perspective

The Scripture is quite clear that no matter what the Christian does, it is to be done to the glory of God. The Apostle Paul in Ephesians 4 and Colossians 1 is also very explicit in stating that the goal of Christian education is to bring every man to the place of "maturity in Christ Jesus." To be *perfect* in the sense that the Scripture speaks of here is to be "complete, lacking nothing" in the sense that Jesus Christ has become completely at home in the totality of a person's life. Colossians 1:15-17 states: "For by him were all things created, that are in heaven, and that are in earth, visible and invisible, whether they be thrones, or dominions, or principalities, or powers: all things were created by him, and for him: and he is before all things, and by him all things consist." Paul is saying specifically to us in the last phrase in verse 17 that in Christ Jesus all things hold together. Without the Person of Jesus Christ, the living Word, and the revelation given to us in the written Word, there is nothing that is a satisfactory core or integrating factor for an individual's life, world view, or philosophy of education.

## Educational Perspective

In Christian education, we need to face the fact that when it comes to the application of the principles upon which Christian education is built, not everyone is actually practicing what they say they are. It is much like the old Negro spiritual—"Everybody talkin' about heaven ain't goin' there." As Gaebelein says, "Everybody talking about Christian education ain't doin' it."[1] Now this is not to say that we are not in any way practicing Christian education. Nevertheless, in respect to a thorough integration of the written Word and the living Word, with the whole of the curriculum as well as the total administrative work of the institution, there certainly is much room for improvement. Many Christian schools—elementary, secondary and college level—are Christian in name only, failing to reflect Harry Blaimires' concept of the "Christian mind" as truly thoroughgoing Christian centers of education.

Professor Gordon Clark speaks of the Christian college where such good things as giving out tracts, holding fervent prayer meetings, going out on gospel teams, opening classes with prayer are the accepted practice; yet the actual instruction is no more Christian than a respectable secular institution. The program is merely a pagan one with a thin covering of Christianity. But the pill, not the coating, does the work.[2] The students are deceived into thinking they have received a Christian education when as a matter of fact, their training has been neither Christian and very well may not even be an education.

Christianity is not a Bible department religion. The principles of the Word of God apply to all subjects and all areas of life and therefore, to some extent, should alter the course of instruction. They should, that is, if these biblical principles are consciously adopted. All knowledge, every question in life, and every truth of the universe finds meaning within the scope of Christianity.

There has been a great deal of talk about the subject of integration in Christian education, but relatively little has been written. Dr. Gaebelein's book, *The Pattern of God's Truth*, certainly stands as a monumental work in this particular area, but this book is probably the only one dealing totally with the subject at hand. I may find myself crawling out on a limb and slowly sawing it off, but as I have attempted to think through this subject I have become convinced of the necessity of looking at some specific areas of implementation. The things that I am going to suggest will in no way be exhaustive in terms of their coverage or comprehensive in the sense that I feel that these are the only factors to be considered. However, I feel that these are the five areas that we need to discover and demonstrate.

## Developing a Biblical Philosophy of Teaching and Learning

If in our teaching we wish to produce behavior change, what should we try to change? Secondly, how should we try to bring about such behavior changes? These two questions are obviously related and, in fact, are two aspects of a more general question which boils down to our view of the nature of man. The Christian believes that although man was created in the image of God, he fell and regeneration or recreation by faith in the finished work of the Lord Jesus Christ is an absolute necessity. Man by his nature is a sinner and needs to be reconciled to a holy God. Based upon this doctrine and other biblical or theological concepts, it would necessarily follow that Christian education must, first of all, be concerned with the individual and his relationship with God, as well as his relationship with his fellowman. It is believed, therefore, that in order for Christian education to even begin, both the teacher and the pupil must be vitally and dynamically related to the Person of Jesus Christ, the Living Word. This is an absolutely essential prerequisite in order for true learning to take place. The emphasis must be on the total development of the pupil's personality in Christian education.

Both Old and New Testament terms that emphasize the teaching-learning process can be categorized under the following headings:

**Learning by experience or observation.** *Lamad*, *yah-dac*, *rah-ah*, *didasko*, and *manthano* also stress the importance of learning by involvement and observing. The student is actively involved, not simply soaking up information.

**Teaching to have results.** *Lamad*, *manthano*, and *didasko* stress the importance of telling so others can do and learn by doing. In the use of *noutheteo*, the result of edification and admonition is by the promotion of spiritual encouragement. The result of teaching in the use of *matheteuo* is to make disciples, a definite target and goal to aim for.

**Direction or instruction.** The importance of proper direction and leading is emphasized in *yah-rah* and *hodegeo*: instruction by warning is expressed in *za-har*; instruction for practical needs is expressed in *chah-cham*; the disciplinary need in training and education is stressed in *paideuo*; the simple giving out of information is seen in *katekeo*; disciples are instructed in *matheteuo*.

## How Is Integration Implemented?
## Model for Implementing Integration

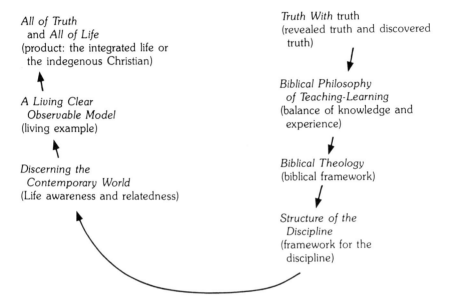

*All of Truth*
and *All of Life*
(product: the integrated life or
the indegenous Christian)

*A Living Clear*
*Observable Model*
(living example)

*Discerning the*
*Contemporary World*
(Life awareness and relatedness)

*Truth With* truth
(revealed truth and discovered
truth)

*Biblical Philosophy*
*of Teaching-Learning*
(balance of knowledge and
experience)

*Biblical Theology*
(biblical framework)

*Structure of the*
*Discipline*
(framework for the
discipline)

**Learning by drawing conclusions and gaining understanding for usefulness.** Been stresses the importance of the student drawing his own conclusions from an incident. Through *sah-kal*, a person can gain understanding on a matter if he will simply ponder or consider the situation very closely. When *suniami* is used, the Christian must be able to obtain understanding by putting many biblical facts together.

**Mind-shaping.** When *shah-nan* is used, it shows the parent giving his child just enough information and in the right manner to influence his understanding. In the use of *noutheteo*, the hearers or readers were written to in order that they might be encouraged or admonished and therefore changed by the instruction.

**Teaching clearly.** Methods of teaching are very important and are seen first in *paratithemi* with the imporance of teaching so the pupil can grasp the meaning; secondly, in *ektithemi* where the method is arranging facts in logical order: and thirdly, in *diermeneuo* where it is very important to explain or interpret the Scriptures.

**Instruction for children.** Verses using *shah-nan*, *lamad* (Deuteronomy 4:10), and *paideuo* all mention the need to instruct children as they are being raised.

**Teaching of God.** *Dianoigo* and *anangello* refer to the way God can open our understanding and reveal to the believer spiritual truth.

Scripture stresses the importance of the pupil's need to be stimulated to learn and then guided into the truth, which is so essential in teaching and learning. God did not intend, for the most part, to dump information upon us and watch us digest it any way we desired. God has purposed that we be taught in such a way that we will want to act upon His teaching. This is the same attitude teachers and parents ought to have when instructing children. Stimulation usually produces action.

In much of our teaching we have emphasized only the nourishing aspect (concepts), and we have done very little, if anything, in terms of exercising our students. As a result, some students have come out with answers to questions that the world is not asking, and as a result they are not capable of competently exercising or applying the concepts learned. They have not been taught "to observe all things" (Matthew 28:20) that God has clearly given in His Word. Christian education requires both an emphasis on impression and expression, nourishing and exercising, the outer factors and the inner factors.

A look at the Book of Romans shows that the first eight chapters are primarily doctrinal and deal with impression. They deal with factual information, doctrinal truth or concepts. But all of this has to be related practically to experience; so Paul takes the last half of the book (chapters 12-16) to practically relate doctrine to real-life experience (competence). Paul does this specifically in the Book of Ephesians, as well as Galatians and Colossians, and James does this throughout the entire book. Martin Luther called the Book of James the epistle of straw because of the emphasis on works. He would not allow the epistle to be included in his canon of Scriptures. But James is loaded with doctrine, and James is attempting to take the doctrinal teaching and relate it specifically to practical real-life experiences. I am convinced that our young people today are screaming for relevancy, and I believe the Word of God is relevant.

What is needed in our approach to teaching and learning is to communicate concepts in a meaningful way, and then in applying and utilizing the skills learned, develop competency.

## Developing a Biblical Theology

The second element is the necessity of developing a biblical theology. Some have tried to define biblical theology as any theology that claims to be based solely on the Bible. As Dr. Charles Ryrie says, "This popular notion makes biblical theology then that which emphasizes the revelational nature of Christianity while minimizing or ignoring rational or philosophical aspects.[3] Though such a theology may be biblical, it is not necessarily biblical theology. Biblical theology, according to Ryrie, deals systematically with the historically conditioned process of the self-revelation of God as deposited in the Bible.[4] First of all, biblical theology views doctrine in its historical context. Often a serious weakness of systematic theology is its failure to view doctrine in its historical context. Frequently systematic theology is that which determines the meaning of a verse or passage rather than the passage molding the system. Viewing doctrine in its historical context, therefore, is the best preventive against the misuse of the theological system. The first step after the exegesis of the text is the development of the doctrinal truths, a biblical theology. The second step is the arrangement of these into a system.

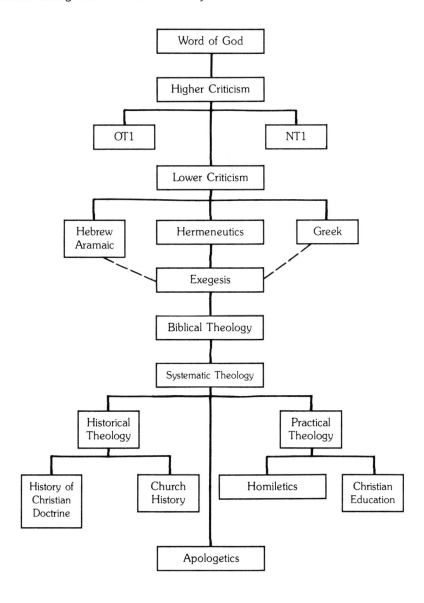

Secondly, biblical theology emphasizes theological structure or concepts and provides for us the basic doctrinal threads that hold all the Bible together. Biblical theology relieves the situation where fundamental doctrines of the faith seem to be so dependent on the testimony of a few isolated proof texts.

Often in the presentation of certain doctrines in systematic theology, the impression is given that these doctrines depend on only one or two biblical texts. The doctrine of inspiration is a good example. Usually two texts are set forth as the New Testament proof of this doctrine: 2 Timothy 3:16 and 2 Peter 1:21. The impression is sometimes left with the student that these are the only two texts that can be used to demonstrate the inspiration of the Scriptures. Ryrie points out that there is no better corrective for such a misconception than a study of the Book of James from the viewpoint of biblical theology. Although James does not make any direct statements concerning inspiration, an investigation of the doctrine of the Word in his epistle reveals beyond any shadow of doubt that there was in his mind a definite substructure of the doctrines of the inspiration and authority of the Word. Ryrie goes on to state that theological structure or substructure is just as valid proof of any doctrine as explicit statements, and no discipline in all the realm of theological studies reveals theological substructure as biblical theology does.[5] There are about fifteen doctrinal concepts that hold all of the Bible together. The following are suggested ways for arranging doctrinal concepts.

1. The Structure of Systematic Theology
   a. Bibliology—The Bible
   b. Theology Proper—God
   c. Soteriology—Salvation
   d. Angelology—Angels
   e. Anthropology—Man
   f. Harmartiology—Sin
   g. Ecclesiology—The church
   h. Eschatology—Last things (Prophecy)
   i. Christology—Christ
   j. Pneumatology—Holy Spirit
2. Doctrinal Summary
   a. Angels
   b. Anthropology
   c. Bibliology
   d. Christology
   e. Covenants
   f. Dispensations
   g. Ecclesiology
   h. Eschatology
   i. God
   j. Holy Spirit
   k. Inspiration

    l. Regeneration
    m. Sin
3. Paul's Theology
    a. The Doctrine of God
    b. Christology—Jesus Christ
    c. The Holy Spirit
    d. Sin
    e. Salvation
    f. The Church
    g. The Christian life
    h. Eschatology—future things

One further aspect of biblical theology, according to Ryrie, is that it fosters a deep appreciation of the grace of God.[6] One who studies, for instance, the theology of the Pentateuch and then Pauline theology, cannot help being impressed with the sharp contrast in the content of revelation. This is true, of course, only if in the study of the theology of the Pentateuch one is careful not to read the New Testament back into the Old. If that is not done, one can only stand in amazement at the fullness of the revelation of the grace of God in Jesus Christ in contrast to that which was revealed in the shadows of the Old Testament. Such a contrast can only bring thankfulness and humility to the heart of the one who lives today, and this awareness ought not only to give him a deeper appreciation of the grace of God, but foster within him a desire to demonstrate the grace of God in a balanced Christian life.

## Discovering the Structure of a Discipline

Thirdly, there is the necessity of discovering the structure of a discipline. We have already talked about structures or substructures as they relate to theology. There is much talk today in the field of education about the structure of a discipline. But what do we mean by this? The structure of a discipline consists at least in part of the body of imposed conceptions (concepts) which define the investigated subject matter of that discipline and control its inquiry. The structure of any discipline is composed of the basic concepts or principles without which you would not have that discipline or which, when put together, form the basic, unchanging framework for that discipline. As Frank Ryan asserts in his book *Exemplars for the New Social Studies*, one-half of what the student is learning today will be obsolete in ten years, and one-half of what he needs to know in ten years has not yet been discovered.[7] This, of course, relates to factual information.

Ryan, along with others, would insist on studying a particular subject from the standpoint of its basic structure so that as new information becomes available and as older ideas become obsolete, they can more readily fit into the structure of the discipline being studied. Ralph Tyler states that the structure of a discipline deals with five basic areas: (1) the questions it deals with; (2) the kind of answers it seeks; (3) the concepts it uses to analyze the field; (4) the methods it uses to obtain data; and (5) the way it organizes its inquiries and findings. This, he says, becomes the means of analyzing the structure of a particular discipline.[8]

Some years ago in a report of the Social Studies Curriculum Committee of the Dalton Schools in New York City, there was developed a list of common elements of the social studies curriculum which they felt could serve as the thread running through the nursery, primary, middle school, and high school to provide the basis for continuity, sequence, and integration in the curriculum. They felt that determining such elements would serve as threads that could be used to weave a more integrated curriculum. The concept of interdependence, they felt, had implications in fields in addition to social studies— art, science, English, physical education, and so on. The value of "the dignity of the worth of every human being" is also a value to be given consideration in other subjects. Thus, these elements can be considered by teachers in other fields as possible threads for weaving a more closely integrated, total school experience, as well as serving to give continuity and sequence, year after year, to the student's experience in the social studies.

The committee went on to urge each member of the faculty to examine the list of elements to see how they either were now or could eventually be brought into their own teaching. The committee felt that emphasis upon such common elements would improve the educational effectiveness of the school by increasing the degree of integration.[9]

# Tentative List of Common Elements in the Social-Studies Curriculum

## Concepts

1. Regarding individual "human nature."
    1.1 There are basic human needs which individuals seek to satisfy. All human beings have certain common needs, but there is variety in their manifestation and attainment.
    1.2 The underlying motivation of a person has strong effects both on him and on others. Among the motives that have had great social consequence are:
    1.21 Struggle for survival.
    1.22 Desire to get ahead, to excel.
    1.23 Quest for security.
    1.24 Struggle for freedom.
    1.25 Desire to attain one's ideals and aspirations for a better life.
    1.3 Much of our talk and action arises from unconscious motivation.
    1.4 Frustrations in human life have serious consequences: compulsive behavior and prejudices limit individual and social effectiveness.

1.5 Although some individual characteristics are largely the result of in-born factors, many components of the "self" and individual personality are formed by experience and training.

1.6 Human beings are almost infinitely teachable. In a sense, "human nature" is being changed every day.

1.7 Ideals can be dynamic in human progress, especially when they are continuously clarified, reinterpreted, and reapplied in changing situations.

2. Regarding man and his physical environment.

2.1 Space is an important dimension in human affairs, for location affects resources, ease of transportation and communication, and many physical conditions of living.

2.2 Time is an important dimension in human affairs, for events have roots and consequences and developments (changes) which require time.

2.3 Climate, land features, and natural resources have profound effects on man. Development, use, and conservation of resources strongly influence his life and future.

2.4 Man can influence his physical environment.

3. Regarding man and his social environment.

3.1 Man forms social institutions and organizations to satisfy his needs.

3.2 People are interdependent.

3.21 The distribution of world resources makes for interdependence.

3.22 Specialization and division of labor make for interdependence.

3.23 The limitations of individual effort make for interdependence.

3.24 Such universal human needs as affection, need to belong to a social group, need for respect from others make for interdependence.

3.3 Social groups develop patterns for group living, thus producing customs, cultures, civilization, and society.

3.4 Increasing knowledge and invention produce ideas and technology that disrupt some previous social arrangements. There is social lag in making adjustments to these disrupting forces. Hence:

3.41 Society involves both change and continuity. Both are inevitable, normal, and serve useful social ends.

3.42 The idea of progress is not a continuous straight-line development. There are some regressions and cessations of advance.

3.43 Some far-reaching and rapid disruptions lead to revolution rather than evolution.

3.431 Intellectual revolution.

3.432 Political revolutions.

3.433 Economic revolutions (the Industrial Revolution).

3.5 An effective social group must provide both for individual needs to be satisfied and for integrated productive group activity. Hence, group organization involves problems of:

3.51 Achieving a balance of freedom and control.
3.52 The place and limits of compromise in dealing with conflicts of personal and social values.
3.53 Ethical and moral standards for the individual and the group.
3.54 The place of religion in individual and group life.
3.55 The place of the arts.
3.56 Democratic social groups in contrast to autocratic, aristocratic, or fascistic ones.

3.6 The organization of social groups for the production and distribution of goods and services has taken several forms and involves serious problems.
3.61 Nomadic life.
3.62 Agriculture and family manufactures.
3.63 Manorial systems.
3.64 Mercantilism.
3.65 Capitalism.
3.66 Socialism.
3.67 Monopoly and oligopoly.

3.7 The organization of political units affects and is affected by economic organization. It has taken several forms and involves serious problems.
3.71 Patriarchal clan or tribe.
3.72 City-state.
3.73 Feudalism.
3.74 Ecclesiastical state.
3.75 Nationalism and imperialism.
3.76 Democracy.
3.77 Communism.
3.78 Facism.

3.8 Social groups can be reshaped to fulfill their functions more adequately.

## Values

1. Attitudes toward self.
   1.1 Growing from self-love to self-respect; acceptance of self, realization of one's own worth.
   1.2 Integrity, honesty and frankness with self; objectively critical of self.
   1.3 Hopefulness for the future.
   1.4 Willingness for adventure; sense of mission, of reformation, of great crusade.
   1.5 Desire to make a productive contribution, not to be a parasite.
2. Attitudes towards others.
   2.1 Respect for the dignity and worth of every human being, regardless of his racial, national, economic or social status.
   2.2 Cherishing variety in people, opinions, acts.
   2.3 Equality of opportunity for all.

2.4 Tolerance, good will, kindliness.

2.5 Desire for justice for all.

3. Attitudes toward social groups to which he belongs.

   3.1 Loyalty to world society and world order.

   3.2 Acceptance of social responsibility.

   3.3 Willingness to submit one's problems to group study and group judgment.

   3.4 Balance of integrity of individual and group participation.

   3.5 Loyalty to social purposes of the group rather than undiscriminating loyalty to whatever the group does.

   3.6 Willingness to work for an abundance of the good things of life for all peoples in the world.

4. Intellectual and aesthetic values.

   4.1 Love of truth, however disconcerting it may be.

   4.2 Respect for work well done, worth of socially directed effort as well as achievement.

   4.3 Freedom of thought, expression, and worship.

   4.4 Love of beauty in art, in surroundings, in the lives of people.

   4.5 Respect for reasonable procedures rather than force as the only proper and workable way of getting along together.

## Skill, Abilities, and Habits

1. In analyzing problems.

2. In collecting facts and other data.

   2.1 Skill in selecting dependable sources of data.

   2.2 Ability to observe carefully and listen attentively.

   2.3 Ability to read critically.

   2.4 Ability to discriminate important from unimportant facts.

   2.5 Ability to take notes.

   2.6 Ability to read charts, graphs, tables, and maps.

3. In organizing and interpreting data.

   3.1 Skill in outlining.

   3.2 Skill in summarizing.

   3.3 Ability to make reasonable interpretations.

4. In presenting the results of study.

   4.1 Skill in writing a clear, well-organized, and interesting paper.

   4.2 Skill in presenting an oral report.

   4.3 Ability to prepare a bibliography.

   4.4 Ability to prepare charts, graphs, tables, and maps.

   4.5 Ability to write a critical book review.

5. Ability to do independent thinking.

6. Ability to analyze argument and propaganda.

7. Ability to participate effectively in group work.

8. Good work habits—planning of time, efficient use of time.

9. Ability to interpret a social situation, to recognize motives and needs of others.
10. Ability to foresee consequences of proposed actions.

"It should also be clear that these elements are not to be viewed as single things, each to be a separate goal of instruction. Good teaching always involves a synthesis of several elements. The same learning experience can contribute to several of these elements at the same time—the child may in this learning experience deepen several concepts, gain a greater concern for certain social values, and acquire increased skill in study. The foregoing elements are suggested threads for the weaving, but the teaching will involve the closely woven fabric. The report will have been of value if it helps to weave a better integrated cloth."⁹

It appears then that when teachers gain an understanding of the structure of a discipline that students learn more effectively and more efficiently the content involved, as well as its relationship to other disciplines. The same is true from a Christian perspective. The discipline concept (D.C.) is related to a concept from biblical theology (B.C.). At this point, the concept from the discipline and the biblical concept are checked and if the D.C. complements the B.C. and is not in conflict, they are in correlation. When the two are woven together into a single larger concept, the step of integration provides us a single biblically integrated concept (B.I.C.). [See chart page 43]

## Discerning the Contemporary World

A fourth area in the implementation of integration in Christian education is the necessity of discerning the contemporary world. The space age dawned suddenly upon a century already beset by two world wars, the introduction of the air age, the era of dictatorships, the jet age, and the atomic age. These and still further developments of the twentieth century have brought both marvelous and yet threatening changes to our civilization.

We have certainly seen that these changes have emphasized the increasing importance of science and technology, but some observers of contemporary life, including numerous scientists, have challenged the wisdom of preoccupation with technical forces, events, and gadgets. The ability to solve the problems of human adjustment to contemporary technical development requires attention, however, to social factors. Even the marvelous computer, "the thinking machine," depends ultimately upon human beings for their programing. Is it not possible that evangelical Christians today still have their heads in the sand and are not fully appraised of what is happening in the world around them? It is very possible to become so buried in biblical truth that one develops a consciousness of the world to come without realizing they are presently in a world that is desperately in need of help. It is possible to become so "heavenly-minded" that we are no earthly good and, as a result of this, are not only incapable of communicating to the needs of the world today but, even more tragically,

MODEL: CORRELATION — INTEGRATION

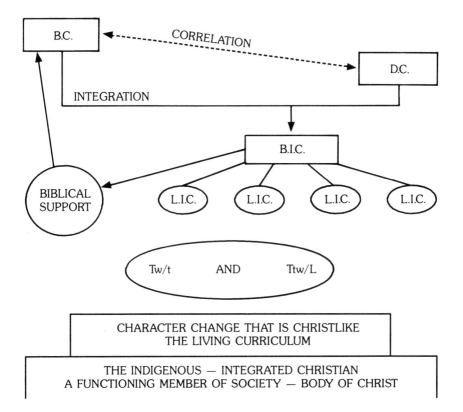

are incapable of equipping our students to be able to relate biblical truth and thus to be able to minister to the needs of a world lost and without Jesus Christ.

Jonathan C. McLendon in his book, *Social Studies in Secondary Education*, makes a number of statements regarding the contemporary social world. These generalizations at least give us a broad overview of what is happening in our world today.

1. The tripling of the world's population in the past two centuries as a result of rising birth rates and generally improved nutrition and medical care has caused a population explosion.
2. A rapidly increasing population has been suggested as a cause for increased social and political problems.
3. For more than a century, a relative decline in American rural population has been accompanied by an accelerating growth in urban areas.
4. The hubbub of life in the city seems to contribute to the greater emotional strain of modern times.
5. More interpersonal relationships are involved in city life than in small towns and rural areas.

6. Industrialization and urbanization bring steadily growing amounts of leisure time to the people involved.
7. The continuing industrial revolution has finally brought about a super-abundant production of goods without having arranged a balancing means of abundant consumption.
8. The demand for recreational facilities created by widespread leisure time has multiplied into a chief type of enterprise in our economy.
9. The very foundations of modern civilization have been shaken by the recurrent danger and actual advent of war in the twentieth century.
10. Technology, trade, exchange problems, and tourist travel have made the world economically and culturally more interdependent.
11. The past century has witnessed tremendous shrinking of the time required for increasingly rapid means of communication.
12. The social effect of a better means of transportation has been to increase the time we spend en route to places to which we otherwise would not go.
13. Though rapid transportation and communication provides a greater number and frequency of contacts with others, much of them are limited to one-time or once-in-a-while contacts.
14. In recent times, knowledge has been accumulated and disseminated at an ever more rapid rate.
15. Whatever may be the philosophical merits of educating the masses, schools have played a key role in the dissemination of knowledge.[10]

## Demonstrating a Clear, Observable Model

The final element in the process of implementing integration in Christian education is the necessity of demonstrating a clear, observable model of the reality of the person of Jesus Christ and the feasibility of the practical implementation of the concept. Two recent instances in working with students that have made me increasingly aware of the necessity that the teacher demonstrate a clear and observable model of the reality of that which the instructor attempts to communicate. In discussing with one student problems relative to faculty members not receiving paychecks on time and obviously facing crucial financial problems, the student responded by saying that essentially his instructor was negating everything that he had been teaching simply by the way the instructor was reacting to an opportunity to demonstrate real faith. I have seen students become so shaken by this kind of reaction that they began to question even the feasibility of being able to live (except in a sterile hospital-type atmosphere) the truths from God's Word that many of us as Bible teachers so clearly expound. Numerous times I have discussed with students the need to trust God and step out by faith. Often the student responds by telling me that after the years in a Christian school, he has not really learned what it is to trust God and be able to step out by faith.

It is interesting that a non-Christian educator such as Ralph Tyler states in connection with the problem of guiding the learner in carrying on a desired behavior that he has found that students commonly observe the teacher's behavior as a model to direct their own. He goes on to say that this is a useful guide if the teacher does frequently demonstrate the behavior the student is expected to acquire, but some teachers do not furnish an observable model of the desired learning behavior.[11] The instructor often only lectures to a class, only demonstrating ways of giving out information rather than showing the student how he goes about solving problems. When students cannot gain a clear picture of what they are to do by observing the teacher, they depend upon other students to show them or tell them. Obviously, this results in frequent misunderstanding of what the student is to do. It is therefore imperative that clear, observable models be provided as a means of guiding the student to produce the desired behavior results.

As children and young people grow up, they often find individuals who seem particularly attractive and seek to emulate them. The young child may begin this process of identification with his mother, following her around the house in an attempt to imitate her behavior. During the years of development other persons, in turn, are objects of identification. This process is one of the ways in which young people learn; and with a variety of constructive personalities available, the outcome can be positive and include the acquisition of attitudes, values, and interests, as well as skills and practices. However, in some of our schools the range of constructive personalities that are close enough to the students to permit attraction and emulation is much too narrow, so that many children and young people find no one on the faculty enough like them to be drawn into identification. This is another consideration for instructional planning that should seek to use all of the important resources, especially the human resources, that can possibly be provided for learning.

## Summary

While it is possible to make a few summary statements regarding this extremely crucial subject of integration in Christian education, I certainly would make no attempt to draw conclusions. A topic such as this can never really be concluded and I can only give a few summary statements of the thoughts that I have attempted to communicate. The primary principle that can be drawn from our brief look at the subject of integration is that learning is most effective when that which is learned is integrated with all of truth and all of life. Ideally this never really ends, for even when you have taught a group about honesty, the process is not complete until the individual is able to bring the concept of honesty into every area of his life. Obviously this is not learning truth in isolation, but attempting to learn truth in relationships and ultimately in integration. Things learned in one situation should not just be correlated or shown to be complementary to another situation, but they should be vitally united and in this way transferred to other areas and even to other cultural settings. If we are truly dealing with principles or concepts, then these principles or concepts will always have the ability of transference crossculturally.

To the extent that the truths presented are integrated with the truth of the written Word and then are transformed into experience both in and out of the classroom, then maturity in Christ developed and the ultimate goal of Christian education is brought to fruition. Christian education valuation is dependent upon integration. Colossians 3:17 says, "Whatsoever ye do in word or deed, do all in the name of the Lord Jesus, giving thanks to God and the Father by him."

## SUMMARY

## INTEGRATION – THE 6 MAJOR CONCEPTS

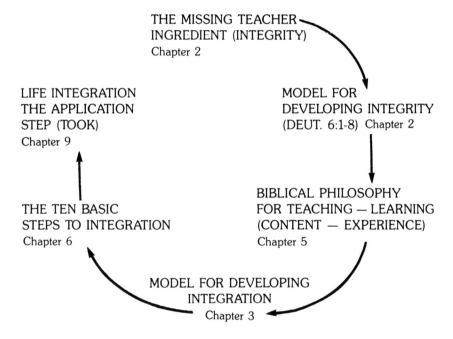

THE MISSING TEACHER
INGREDIENT (INTEGRITY)
Chapter 2

LIFE INTEGRATION
THE APPLICATION
STEP (TOOK)
Chapter 9

MODEL FOR
DEVELOPING INTEGRITY
(DEUT. 6:1-8) Chapter 2

THE TEN BASIC
STEPS TO INTEGRATION
Chapter 6

BIBLICAL PHILOSOPHY
FOR TEACHING – LEARNING
(CONTENT – EXPERIENCE)
Chapter 5

MODEL FOR DEVELOPING
INTEGRATION
Chapter 3

1. Frank E. Gaebelein, *The Pattern of God's Truth* (Chicago: Moody Press, 1968), p. 15.

2. Gordon H. Clark, *A Christian Philosophy of Education* (Grand Rapids, MI: Wm. B. Eerdmans, 1946), pp. 208-210.

3. Charles Ryrie, *Biblical Theology of the New Testament* (Chicago: Moody Press, 1959), p.12.

4. Ibid.

5. Ibid., p. 22.

6. Ibid., p. 23.

7. Frank L. Ryan, *Exemplars for the New Social Studies: Instruction in the Elementary Schools* (Englewood Cliffs, N.J.: Prentice-Hall, 1971), p. 15.

8. Ralph Tyler, *Basic Principles of Curriculum and Instruction* (Chicago: University of Chicago Press, 1969), pp. 89-94.

9. Ibid., pp. 89-94.

10. Johathan C. McLendon, *Social Studies in Secondary Education* (New York: Macmillan Co., 1965), pp. 3-9.

11. Tyler, pp. 76, 77.

Chapter 4

# The Distinctive Philosophy of Curriculum

## Introduction

Since Christian education is distinctive, then it is not legitimate to have the same integrating factor as would be found in a manmade system. But how then do Christian educators handle the relationship between content and experience in the development of curriculum philosophy?

Is it not sufficient to have a God-centered or Bible-centered education? Certainly if God and the Bible are not at the center, it can never be Christian. It is believed, however, that God never meant that the written Word and the living Word should be separated. The integrating factor in the individual's Christian life obviously should be the living Word, Jesus Christ, who is "the same yesterday, and today, and for ever" (Hebrews 13:8). With Jesus Christ at the center, there is a nonterminating core and all of life is integrated around a Person who never changes. But the living Word can only be known through the revelation of the written Word, which is the integrating factor in Christian education for discovered truth.

A God-centered or Bible-centered approach is not incorrect, but does not clearly show the relationship of Jesus Christ, the living Word, and the Bible, the written Word. In stating that the educational philosophy is Word-centered, it is believed that this then shows the balance between the outer and inner factors, the Bible and Jesus Christ (John 1:1-4; 10:30; 8:58; Exodus 3:14).

To the extent that the truths presented are integrated with the truth of the written Word and then are transformed into experience both in and out of the classroom, to this extent is maturity in Christ developed and the ultimate goal of Christian education brought to fruition. This concept is illustrated in the following diagram by Dr. LeBar.[1]

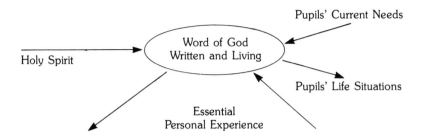

Thus, the center of Christian education, and specifically the area of curriculum, does not change with every new idea on the educational market, nor is it centered in sinful human life, but rather in the One who is divine life Himself, eternal life, fullness of life, the living Word revealed by the written Word. It is not the book but the Person revealed in the book who gives the dynamic, vitality, and power needed in a distinctive Christian philosophy of curriculum.

## Definition of Curriculum

The transition from a Word-centered Christian, theistic worldview to actual teaching practice is bridged by the curriculum. The word *curriculum* is derived from the Latin *currere*, which means "to run" and in ancient Rome referred to "running on a racecourse." The dictionary commonly defines *curriculum* as a "course of study . . . or a body of courses offered by an educational institution. . . ." Smith, Stanley, and Shores have described this concept of curriculum:

> A sequence of potential experiences as set up by the school for the purpose of disciplining children and youth in group ways of thinking and eating . . . a set of educational objectives, a body of subject matter, a list of exercises or activities to be performed, a way of determining whether or not the objectives have been reached, a kind of control the teacher is expected to exercise over learners—these things comprise the curriculum.[2]

Whether we are referring to elementary, secondary, higher education, or church education, the curriculum may be defined narrowly as the courses offered, or broadly as all the experiences offered by the school, or the particular experiences a given student has while in school. Traditionally the course or curriculum was considered the body of content that the student covered in his educational progress. More recently, the term connotes the activities of the student as he is engaged in various experiences which involve content.[3]

> In a scriptural orientation, the "curriculum" may be defined as those activities in relation to authoritative content that are guided or employed by Christian leadership in order to bring pupils one step nearer to maturity in Christ.[4]

However, the question of the center, the integrating force, becomes crucial in structuring a curriculum. As Christians, we must see that an authoritative content and personal experience are paramount to the total development of the personality within the framework of the Christian, theistic worldview.

Can Christians accomplish their aims and objectives in a curriculum that is man-centered? Some have proposed that only a God-centered curriculum can be Christian: and this is absolutely correct, for without God an atheistic worldview is all that remains. However, the only revelation of God and His Son which provides for the restoration of fellowship between Creator and creature is the written Word of God, and He never meant that the written Word should be separated from the living Word.

In chapter 5 on teaching-learning we will see that education must be both product and process. It is a balance of both content and experience, truth and life. Apart from the written Word (content) the living Word (experience) can never by known. Thus, the concept of a God-centered and Bible-centered approach are drawn together as intended by God in the clearer concept of a Word-centered approach.

In planning, carrying out, and evaluating instructional programs at any level of education, a series of basic questions must be answered.

1. What educational purposes should the school seek to attain?
2. What educational experiences can be provided that are likely to attain these purposes?
3. How can these educational experiences be effectively organized?
4. In what order or sequence shall these educational experiences be offered?
5. How shall we determine whether these purposes are being attained?
6. Who shall determine the answers to these questions?
7. By what procedure shall decisions on these questions be made?[5]

When these seven questions have been answered and the answers implemented, the instructional program (curriculum) of the school or church has been both defined and developed.

## Concept-Competence Curriculum
*The Subject Matter-Experience Curriculum in Education*

Consistent with our commitment to "discipling" or developing individuals who have a balance of belief and behavior and our commitment to a biblical philosophy of teaching and learning, a balance of content and experience, impression and expression, nourishing and exercising, we are suggesting a balanced perspective of concept and competence. This approach is solidly based in God's inscripturated revelation as given to us in the written Word but also is not losing sight of the life-relatedness as demonstrated in the Living Word, Jesus Christ.

| Subject Matter Curriculum | Experience Curriculum |
|---|---|
| second hand observation— | first hand observation— |
| passive involvement | active involvement |
| imposed experience | integrated experience |
| atomistic approach | wholistic approach |
| content-oriented | process-oriented |
| uniformity of learning | diversity of learning |
| teacher active-student passive | teacher and student active |
| achievement-normative scale | achievement-individual scale |

Another approach to curriculum has been suggested by Lewis Mayhew, who proposes a general education based on selected experiences. Mayhew proposes that every student should:

1. have the opportunity to engage in independent study in which he sets his own goals and proceeds at his own rate, decides when he is finished, and feels free to use or not use professional resources of the institution;
2. learn in large and impersonal situations;
3. learn to function in small groups;
4. have a relationship with an adult professional person which is sustained over a period of time;
5. have a sustained off-campus experience of some sort;
6. have the opportunity to know intimately a culture or subculture different from his own;
7. be required to make a sustained effort over a prolonged period of time on a particular task;
8. have the opportunity to engage in a number of brief ad hoc activities which have the same curricular value as longer and more sustained efforts;
9. enjoy, unpenalized, opportunities to engage in play for his own personal satisfactions;
10. have opportunities to gain deeper understanding of his own emotions and those of others;
11. have a chance to learn by using some of the newer media;
12. have an aesthetically creative experience regardless of the level of his performance.[6]

The concept-competence curriculum, from a Christian perspective, attempts to integrate the student's cognitive development with the development of his total personality in relation to a thoroughly biblical world and life-view for the purpose of producing character change that demonstrates maturity in Jesus Christ. This approach to curriculum is solidly based in and dependent upon God's revelation, but not without reasonably and rationally tying it to reality.

## The Ten Most Crucial Questions in Regard to Curriculum
1.  What is the basic purpose or philosophy of curriculum?
    Without an adequate conception of what we mean or include in our con-

cept of curriculum, we lack a rudder to give us theoretical and practical direction.

2a.  What is our understanding of the philosophy of teaching?
An adequate conception of the role or function of the teacher as a motivator, stimulator, or guide to cause the student to personally become meaningfully involved in the process will greatly affect our concept of curriculum.

2b.  What is our understanding of the philosophy of learning?
The role of the student as an active rather than passive participant in the process is also vital to our approach to curriculum and the process of learning.

3.  What are the "operationally defined" or behaviorally stated objectives?
As our philosophy gives us direction, our goals tell us specifically what we are moving toward.

4.  What is the basic structure of the subject or content areas to be taught?
(The structure of the discipline is made up of the basic concepts which form the framework for that discipline, and that structure does not change.) With the rapid information explosion we cannot possibly teach all the facts, but we need to give students a basic framework to which they can continually add information as it becomes available.

5.  What are the relevant world, national, and community needs and problems we must be aware of?
This will require that our curriculum planning be flexible in order to keep it fresh and relevant to meet the needs of our students.

6.  What educational experiences do we want our students to have in the school classroom as well as in the community?
Our curriculum will of necessity need to be wedded to real life and so will demand not only knowing, but applying and utilizing what the students know.

7.  How will these educational experiences be organized?
This will require careful planning of teaching strategies for both in and out of the classroom.

8.  What horizontal (classroom) and vertical (grade level) organization will be utilized?
My recommendation would be a 4-4-4 (grades 1-4, 5-8, 9-12) vertical organization utilizing both homogeneous and heterogeneous multi-age level groupings in an integrated or modified open concept approach.

9.  What procedures will be utilized to evaluate the degree of accomplishment of our behaviorally stated objectives?
The watchword today is accountability; so we will need to determine our successes and failures. Educational evaluation is always on the basis of educational objectives; so the clearer we have stated our objectives, the more accurately we can evaluate.

10.  By what means will we proceed to train teachers to implement in practice the theoretical model of curriculum we have established?

This undoubtedly will be our most difficult problem, unless the teacher training institutions quickly provide instructors and courses where this creative, innovative model is implemented.

1. LeBar, p. 206.

2. Othanel Smith, William O. Stanley, and J. Harlan Shores, *Fundamentals of Curriculum Development*, rev. ed. (New York: Harcourt, Brace, and World, Inc., 1957), p. 3.

3. LeBar, p. 203.

4. Ibid.

5. Tyler, p. 1.

6. Lewis B. Mayhew, *Contemporary College Students and the Curriculum* (Atlanta: Southern Regional Ed. Bd., 1969), p. 33.

# Chapter 5

# The Distinctive Philosophy
# of Teaching-Learning

All the history of education can be plotted on a single continuum with two extremes. On the one extreme stands Johann Friedrich Herbart, with an emphasis on content, while on the other stands the extreme of John Dewey, with an emphasis on experience. To put this into more contemporary thinking, Herbart would see the teacher as primarily a disseminator of information, while John Dewey believed the teacher to be primarily a facilitator of learning.

Which is more important: the process of becoming an educated man, or the product of actually being educated? This is the dilemma that the history of education provides when we attempt to develop our philosophy of teaching-learning. Though the Latin root of the word *education* contains the concept both of an infilling process as well as a drawing out process (the emphasis on impression and expression, nourishing and exercising), apparently educators through the centuries have not fully accepted this. In addition, there has not always been agreement as to the necessity of balance in relationship to content and experience, the impression and expression; nor has there been agreement as to the logical order of these two elements.

From a biblical perspective the Word of God seems to say that impression minus expression leads to depression. In other words, the Bible tells us that the imparting of the truth minus the expression of it leads to spiritual depression. Many would say that if we are teaching the Bible, then we are teaching the right thing, and it really does not make any difference how we give it out. I have had people tell me that to qualify as a teacher, you only need a knowledge of your subject matter and an enthusiasm in actually presenting it. I certainly believe that these two are very essential, but apparently these alone do not fulfill the criteria that the Word of God gives to us regarding effective teaching and learning.

It is possible to do the right thing in the wrong way. There are always those who respond and say, "But don't you believe Isaiah 55:11?" Yes, I believe it, but not the way most people apply it. So many use that verse as a cop-out, thinking that all they have to do is somehow spray the Word of God at people and it will not return void. If that be the case, then it would be much better for us to buy "gospel blimps" or to engage in some sort of mass saturation of areas through radio or television to get the Word of God out to people as quickly as possible. However, just as the cults so often do with verses, we have taken verse 11 completely out of the context of Isaiah 55. Isaiah begins by saying, if you are thirsty and you are hungry, and you don't have any money, come, buy and eat. In verse 2 he talks about "hearkening diligently unto me [the Lord]," while in verse 3 he talks about inclining "your ear, and come unto me: hear, and your soul shall live." In verse 6 he says "Seek ye the Lord while he may be found, call ye upon him while he is near." In verse 7 he says, "Let the wicked forsake his way, and the unrighteous man his thoughts: and let him return unto the Lord." Then in verses 8 and 9 he gives the words that are so often quoted: "For my thoughts are not your thoughts, neither are your ways my ways, saith the Lord. For as the heavens are higher than the earth, so are my ways higher than your ways, and my thoughts than your thoughts." These verses give us the context for verse 11. Now Isaiah says, "So shall my word be that goeth forth out of my mouth: it shall not return unto me void, but it shall accomplish that which I please, and it shall prosper in the thing whereto I sent it."

Isaiah was never implying that all we needed to do was to somehow get the Word out so that people could hear it, and then it would not return void. He said that as we teach and present the Word of God, we must strive to make people hungry, thirsty, and willing to seek the Lord, willing to incline their ear unto the Lord, and willing to forsake their wicked way by creating the appropriate climate or atmosphere which enables the Word of God to be used in lives and bring about positive results. I do not believe that Isaiah had any thought of the Word of God returning void in the sense that it was drawing people either to the Lord or driving people away from the Lord. The negative was not in the mind of the writer.

Some time ago someone tried to explain Isaiah 55:11 by comparing it to the miracle that our Lord performed at the marriage feast at Canaan. Hiding God's Word in our minds or in our hearts is like pouring water into empty water jugs. As the water was miraculously turned into wine by our Lord, likewise when the Word of God enters the mind the Lord miraculously changes it and causes the student to grasp and understand it, as well as making it a part of his life. This is an interesting analogy, but unfortunately it does not hold water in relationship to what the Word of God says to us about teaching-learning.

One of the first places we can go for enlightenment on this is the writings of the apostle Paul. As we consider contemporary ideas of infilling, drawing out; impression, expression; nourishing, exercising; content, experience; product, process, we discover that most of Paul's New Testament epistles follow the basic pattern of true education. In the Book of Romans the first eight chapters emphasize the content and give us the doctrine we need to know. Chapters 9-11 deal with the dispensational aspect of the book in relationship to Israel's past, present and future, while subsequent chapters take the doctrinal truth of the first part of the book and apply it to practical Christian living. The Book of Galatians—the first two chapters being personal, 3 and 4 being doctrinal, and 5 and 6 being practical—again basically follows this same pattern. Colossians with its four chapters, also follows this pattern, with the first two chapters being more doctrinal, the emphasis on content, while chapters 3 and 4 deal with practical instructions, emphasizing the experience aspect.

Ephesians is probably the most outstanding example of Paul's educational approach, with the first three chapters giving the believer's exalted position (seated with Christ in the heavenlies), while chapters 4-6 emphasize the practical outworking of this in terms of Christian living or experience. In Ephesians 4:1 Paul says, "I beseech you that ye walk worthy of the vocation wherewith ye are called." We see from Paul's use of the Greek word *axios*(worthy) that we should be walking in a manner that is in balance or equal weight with the position that we have with Christ in the heavenlies. In the first three chapters, Paul uses the word "walk" only twice (both times in chapter 2). The first time (2:2) he talks about our former walk, the way we used to walk before we came to know Jesus Christ as Savior. In verse 10 Paul talks about being "created in Christ Jesus unto good works, which God hath before ordained that we should walk in them." This focuses on the way we should be walking (future). It is interesting that the emphasis on walking in the present is not found until we get to Ephesians 4:1. (One commentator says that the words that describe the book of Ephesians are *sit, walk,* and *stand.* Not only is that impossible—it is illogical and does not follow the pattern that Paul has given to us.) The apostle Paul says that first of all you need to understand that you are *seated* in the heavenlies, and then you need to learn to *stand* in this exalted position. The result of this is that you ought to be able to effectively *walk* in relationship to the Christian life.

Even in Paul's epistles we have the logical order or pattern we need. First of all, the truth of the Word of God must be effectively taught not only in the sense that the person is able to grasp or understand it, but there must also be an emphasis on the practical application or outworking of this in terms of our daily Christian walk. The apostle Paul is saying that it is first of all impression and then expression, nourishing and then exercising, biblical content and then biblical living. To put it still another way, the written Word must be presented to the individual so that it might become the living Word in the individual's life.

Next we want to examine the biblical words for teaching and learning found in both the Old and New Testaments. There are twenty-five of these words, eleven found in the Old Testament (Hebrew) and fourteen found in the New Testament (Greek). First we will examine some of the words in relationship to teaching-learning theory. Then we will summarize all twenty-five of these by looking at the words themselves, the key verse(s), the key word to summarize it, and the key concept for the teaching process as well as the learning process.

The most common word for teaching and learning in the Old Testament is *Lamad*. *Lamad* does not mean a mere dumping of facts or information on the subject, but to stimulate the student to be able to imitate or apply in his life action that which he has come to know. This kind of learning means to become experienced in the sense that a person becomes accustomed to something and subjectively assimilates it into his life. The word is found in Deuteronomy 5:1, where Moses talks about hearing "the statutes and judgments which I speak in your ears this day, that ye may learn them, and keep, and do them." Earlier in Deuteronomy (4:10) Moses reminded the children of Israel how the Lord told him to gather the people together, "and I will make them hear my words, that they may learn to fear me all the days that they shall live upon the earth, and that they may teach their children." An interesting concept that comes up continually through the Book of Deuteronomy, and probably is best seen in Deuteronomy 6:1-3, is that Moses emphasized to the children of Israel that they should teach in such a way that the people would be able to observe and to do that which they have learned.

A very familiar verse of Scripture that uses the Hebrew word *Lamad* is Psalm 32:8; "I will instruct thee and teach thee in the way which thou shalt go; I will guide thee with mine eye." An interesting insight from verse 8 is that the instruction here is in relationship not to what they should know—that is assumed—but in the way that they should go in terms of specific behavior in their life. Isaiah 26:9 talks about the Lord desiring them and with his Spirit seeking them, "for when thy judgments are in the earth, the inhabitants of the world will learn righteousness." This evidently is not just learning the concept of righteousness, but learning it to such an extent that it is assimilated into their life so they are living what they have come to learn.

*Shah-nan* is a very unusual word for teaching-learning found in Deuteronomy 6:7. It is used only once in this teaching or didactic sense, but certainly used most graphically in this extremely important passage. The word means to whet the appetite or senses for learning: "you shall sharpen your children's minds, cut deep into their understanding that they may know me . . ." (author's translation).

*Didasko* is the most common word for teaching-learning in the New Testament, and the focus is on the activity of teaching. This word does not leave out the content or the doctrinal truth, but focuses more on the process or the activity enabling the person to actually learn. Ephesians 4:21 uses this word: "If so be that ye have heard him, and have been taught by him, as the truth is in Jesus." It is also used in Colossians 1:28: "whom we preach, warning every man, and teaching every man in all wisdom; that we may present every man perfect (complete) in Christ Jesus." Colossians 3:16 also uses the word *didasko*:

"Let the word of Christ dwell in you richly in all wisdom; teaching and admonishing (or mind-shaping) one another in psalms and hymns and spiritual songs, singing with grace in your hearts to the Lord." Here the word is used in relationship to the word of Christ that is indwelling in you, in the sense that it is permeating the whole life. The outworking of this will be wisdom or the practical application of knowledge. Here the "teaching" mentioned is emphasizing the process or the activity, while the word "admonishing" is another of the Greek words which focuses on the aspect of mind shaping.

An interesting note is that Colossians 3:16 talks about the word of Christ indwelling, while Ephesians 3:17 talks about the fact that Christ dwells in you in the sense that He dwells deep down in you heart, becoming completely at home in every area or sphere of your life. Thus we see that the Word of Christ and the Person of Christ as well as the Spirit of Christ need to become controlling factors in our life.

*Paideuo* is the verb form of the Greek word for child and literally means "child training." It is also translated in the King James Version as chastened and means to give guidance, to instruct or train in the sense of child training or child raising. Also it refers to the corrective or disciplinary aspect of education, and in Hebrews 12 is coupled together with the extreme aspect of discipline in the word "scourging."

*Noutheteo* literally means "mind shaping" and means to train by word of encouragement. It can take on the negative meaning and emphasize the warning or reproving aspect, but it is generally translated as admonition. This word is used by Jay Adams in the development of his concept of nouthetic counseling.

*Katekeo* literally means "to din into the mind or the ear" and is the Greek word from which we get our English word *catechism*. *Matheteuo* means to make a disciple, and interestingly enough is used only in the Gospels and in the Book of Acts. It is never found in the noun or the verb form in any of the Epistles. This causes some concern for those who feel that there is too much emphasis on discipling today, but I think the answer is simply that the Gospels and the Book of Acts emphasize the purpose that God had in mind, while the Epistles describe for us the process that actually is involved in making disciples.

*Paratithemi* means to put something before someone in the sense that they are able to mentally grasp it, while *ektithemi* means to set forth, expound, or explain the facts in logical order. *Suniami* means to comprehend or gain insight by putting the facts together, so that they can be useful. A key passage is Ephesians 5:17, where Paul tells the Ephesian believers not to be mindless or stupid, but to understand or synthesize the will of God. This is done when the biblical facts as well as the information from the circumstances are put together, and in so doing you arrive at an understanding of God's will for your life.

*Hodegeo* means to lead, guide or cause someone to discover practical doctrinal truth. This is the word that is used in John 16:13 when Jesus tells us that He is not going to leave us as orphans, but He will send the Comforter, the One who is called alongside of us to lead or guide us into an understanding of spiritual truth. In Acts 8 when Philip comes and "joins" (literally, fastens or glues) himself to the chariot and hears the eunuch reading from Isaiah, he asks if he understands what he is reading. The response of the eunuch is, "How can I, except some man should guide me?" This Scripture shows us that in the teaching-learning process there is of necessity the leading, guiding ministry not only of the divine teacher—the Holy Spirit—but also the human instrumentality.

## TEACHING AND LEARNING
### Bible Words For the Teaching-Learning Process

| Word | Key Verse | Key Word | Teaching Process | Learning Process |
|---|---|---|---|---|
| LAMAD | Deut. 5:1 | assimilating | not dumping information, but stimulating to imitation | create a response in action, become experienced, assimilation |
| BIN | Neh. 8:7,8 Dan. 9:23 | discriminating | distinguish, draw conclusions, explain alternatives | understand, so as to apply truth learned |
| ALAPH | Prov. 22:25 | cleaving | to adopt, to hold to truth by experience | make familiar, to hold or adopt as one's own |
| YAH-DAC | Exodus 10:2 Joshua 23:14 | observing | to know by experience | learn by one's own observation |
| DAH-VAR | Jer. 28:16 | proclaiming | speak, say, proclaim | simply learning |
| YAH-RAH | 1 Sam. 12:23 | directing | to direct by words, example | directive learning |
| ZAH-HAR | Psalm 19:11 | warning | to illuminate the mind, instruction, warning | replacing darkness with light ignorance with knowledge |
| CHAH-KAM | Prov. 8:33 | application | to apply instruction to practical needs of life | personal application of principles in daily life |
| SHAH-NAN | Duet. 6:7 | sharpening skills | to whet the appetite, to make a deep impression | gaining a deep understanding |
| RAH-AH | Prov. 6:6 | observing carefully | see a need and make provision, provide example and illustration | learn by observation |
| DIDASKO | Eph 4:21 | involving activity | the activity of teaching | ability to teach others also |
| PAIDEUO | Eph. 6:4 | instructing | guiding by instruction and discipline | growing in maturity |
| NOUTHETEO | Col. 1:28 | mind-shaping | shaping the mind by encouragement, reproof | renewed thoughts and attitudes |
| KATEKEO | Rom. 2:18 | communicating | to dip into the mind, oral communication of fact | repetition (catechism), recitation |
| MATHETEUO | Matt. 28:19 | discipline | instruction in loyalty and devotion to a person and his beliefs | a follower who is a leaner |
| OIKODOMEO | I Cor. 8:1 | edifying | promote growth and maturity, learning through love | maturity |

| | | | | |
|---|---|---|---|---|
| MANTHANO | Matt. 11:29 | experiencing | provide pattern, practice and experience | personally appropriate in personal experience |
| PARATITHEMI | I Tim. 1:18 | comprehending | set forth clearly and plainly | to mentally grasp |
| EKTITHEMI | Acts 11:4 | expounding | to present facts in logical order, explain, expound | recital of facts |
| DIERMENEUO | Luke 24:27 | interpreting | to interpret, unfold, open up, translate spiritual truth | discovery through explanation |
| DIANOIGO | Luke 24:31 | opening | to open minds and hearts to spiritual truth | the opening of ears, eyes and heart to spiritual understanding |
| SUNEMI | Eph. 5:17 | understanding | to put together as as to understand | assimilate so as to apply facts |
| HODEGEO | Acts 8:31 | guiding | cause to discover practical truth, to guide or lead to understanding | understand so as to apply truth |
| ANANGELLO | John 16:13 | proclaiming | to dispense factual truth, proclaim, report, declare | to verbally respond |

Educators generally are in agreement that teachers teach as they were taught. The Scripture gives to us some interesting insight along these lines in Luke 6:39, 40 as well as in Matthew 10:24, 25. The Luke 6 passage literally translated says, "Can one blind person guide another; shall they not both fall into the ditch? A disciple is not above his teacher, but everyone having been perfected will be as his teacher." The word for "perfected" is the same as is found in Ephesians 4:12 and literally means to equip a person. It is also used to describe the mending of a broken net, a doctor setting broken bones, or the complete outfitting of a ship in preparation for a long voyage. The Scripture is saying that as the teacher is, so the student will become.

Are there any specific passages of Scripture that can provide the steps or model that would be involved in the teaching-learning process? Certainly Deuteronomy 6 puts the emphasis on teaching in such a way that people can act upon what they have been taught. Moses outlines the steps involved in ultimately producing the desired result—namely, the Word of God becoming the controlling factor in the actions, attitudes, private and public life of the individual. Matthew 28 and the words of our Lord emphasize that teaching should be done in such a way that the people might observe the teachings that they have come to know.

Probably 1 Thessalonians 1 is one of the most complete passages dealing with the subject of the model teacher and model teaching. It provides some valuable insights. In verse 2 Paul emphasizes necessary preparation ("making mention of you in our prayers"). In verse 5 he adds that the gospel came "not to you in word only, but also in power, and in the Holy Ghost, and in much assurance; as ye know what manner of men we were among you for your sake." Then Paul says the Thessalonian believers became followers (literally, imitators) of him and, as a result, of the Lord, and "received the word in much affliction, with joy of the Holy Ghost." The result of this is seen in verses 7 and 8, where he says they became "ensamples" (literally a model, example or pattern) to all the believers in Macedonia and Achaia. "But also in every place your faith to God-ward is spread abroad; so that we need not to speak any thing." Apparently Paul is emphasizing that we must be concerned not only with the content that is being taught, but *how* it is taught, as well as the life of the individual who is actually doing the teaching.

The clearest step-by-step biblical model for teaching-learning is found in Colossians 1:9, 10. The first thing that Paul stresses is the *recognition of need* in relationship to the people he is going to be teaching. "For this cause we also, since the day we heard it, do not cease to pray for you." The Colossian believers did not face a serious spiritual problem. In fact, earlier in the chapter Paul gave thanks for their faith and hope and love. He was thrilled at the progress that they had made spiritually, and used this as a starting point for his teaching ministry to them, a ministry which followed his *preparation in prayer.* "We do not cease to pray for you." Though this is not the same word that Paul uses in 1 Thessalonians 1 and 5, the emphasis is very similar. Paul's concern for them caused him to pray without allowing long intermissions between his praying. The issue for the apostle Paul was not, "How much time do you spend in prayer?" but rather, "How long has it been since the last time you prayed?" Prayer was not simply a specific period of time set aside *every once in a while,* but a characteristic of his life, especially in relationship to the people he was trying to teach.

The third thing stressed in Colossians 1 was the *information* or the *knowledge.* He desired that they might be "filled with the knowledge of his [God's] will." The word for "filled" is the same as is found in Ephesians 5:18 in relationship to the Holy Spirit. It stresses the fact that we need to be filled (that is, controlled) by the knowledge of God's will. This is not primarily an emphasis on quantity, but on a quality of life that comes as a result of our being controlled by God. The word for knowledge that Paul uses here is *epignosis* and probably relates the *oida* or intellectual knowledge to the subjective or the experiential level of our life.

The fourth thing Paul stressed was the *implication* of this as seen in *wisdom.* He stresses that they might be "filled with the knowledge of his will in all wisdom and spiritual understanding." "Wisdom" is the practical application of the knowledge you already have, while spiritual "understanding" is the synthesis or putting together of the biblical facts to gain the insight that is necessary. It is one thing to know that God is immutable, that His character never changes. It is another thing to understand the implications of this and to be able to say, "Thank you, God, that you can be trusted," believing that whatever He promises He will do.

The fifth thing that Paul emphasizes involves *implementation.* Paul says we are to walk in a manner that is worthy of the Lord. First of all, this walk refers to walking around, and so emphasizes the total sphere of life. The word for "worthy," *axios*, stresses the need for a balance between what you know and what you are actually doing. In Ephesians 4:1, probably the clearest example of this word, Paul stresses that our walk should be in balance or in equal weight with our position (seated with Christ in the heavenlies.)

Sixth, Paul focuses on *multiplication* or *fruit*: "being fruitful in every good work." Apparently, proper preparation and proper instruction in the Word of God will produce fruit in our lives, with the final result being seen in the seventh step of *maturation* or *growth*. Here Paul is emphasizing the idea of "increasing in the knowledge of God." Again Paul uses the word *epignosis* to stress that our developing understanding of God should result in growth in the area of experiencing His Word in our life.

The apostle Paul stresses that true learning begins with facts about God and ends with an increased knowledge of God; but the real goal is to produce godliness in our life. True learning begins with information about God's plan and purpose and ends with the knowledge of his Person; but again the ultimate goal is to produce a "perfect" man. The Bible is trying to communicate to us the fact that learning just for the sake of learning, to amass knowledge, is not acceptable. The Bible is saying to us that true learning is for living.

This is also seen in Hebrews 5:11-14. "Concerning whom we have much to say and hard to interpret, since you have become dull in your hearings. For indeed though by this time you ought to be teachers, you have need that someone teach you again the rudiments of the beginning of the oracles of God. You have become as those having need of milk and not of solid food. For everyone partaking of milk is without experience of the Word of righteousness, for he is an infant" (author's translation). The King James Version of verse 13 says that they were "unskillful in the word of righteousness," and this is often interpreted to mean that they did not have the ability to properly understand, interpret and teach the Word. Even though this may be involved, the true meaning of "unskillful" is that they were lacking experience in relationship to the Word of righteousness. In other words, they knew the truth, but they were not experiencing it in their daily life.

There are at least two dangers that we face in our teaching. One is the danger of leading individuals to only verbalize their Christianity. We must recognize that verbalizing (expression) is the test or proof of teaching, but living (actualizing) is the proof of real learning. Our goal should not be to simply prepare students to verbalize their Christianity, but to actualize it in their life on a day to day basis.

The second danger is to lead people to only have an experience or emotional catharsis in relationship to the Word. We must understand that the goal of Christian education as given to us in the Word is not just to come to know the truth, but to implement the truth, to become truth. Moses would say: *teach to observe to do*. Jesus would say *teach to observe*, while Paul would emphasize the fact that we should *teach* in order that people might be able to *walk* in a manner that is *worthy* of their calling.

Though it is true that John 1:14 refers specifically to the Person of the Lord Jesus Christ, there is a sense in which the principle of this verse must still be applied to us today. "The Word became flesh." Our educational system and approach to teaching-learning must be solidly based upon and centered in the Word, both the written Word and the living Word. Let us never forget that the ultimate test of Christian education is not just academic excellence, but rather character change and Christ likeness. In Christian education, true teaching-learning is always for the purpose of living more Christ-like lives and demonstrating Biblical wisdom.

# Chapter 6

# How Do We Integrate?
# The Model Demonstrated

Dr. Frank Gaebelein in *The Pattern of God's Truth* does an excellent job of making the Christian educator a "believer" regarding the necessity of integration. However, the majority of those who read the book come away more convinced than ever that they ought to be integrating but are unable to put a handle on the process. Francis Schaeffer in his writings does not try to convince us of the necessity of integrating. He simply integrates, bringing every truth and concept into harmony and proper relationship with the truth of the Word of God. Gaebelein *says* integrate and Francis Schaeffer simply *does* it, but the question that seems to go unanswered for most Christian teachers at every level is "How do we integrate?"

In chapter 3 we defined correlation and integration, truth with truth and truth with life. We have further explained in chapter 2 how the teacher is such a vital part of the integrative process and in chapter 3 what specifically is concept with concept integration. In this chapter we will work specifically on the model for true integration and in this way will turn the theory into practice.

The first step is to discover or determine the discipline concept (D.C.) and then to state the related biblical concept (B.C.). In this first step of correlation the two concepts, the D.C. and the B.C. relate alongside of each other and yet they must be complementary or in harmony with one another. If the concept from the discipline cannot be brought into harmony with the biblical concept, then the D.C. must either be totally rejected or be modified to make it consistent with the Word of God. An example of this might be the concept that "man is the highest form of animal creation." This statement is not consistent with the Word of God. Genesis 1 and 2 clearly state that man was not created the same as the animals, but was in fact created in the image of God. There may be some debate or discussion on the use of the word animal, for it would be said that man is not vegetable or mineral but neither is man the

MODEL: CORRELATION — INTEGRATION

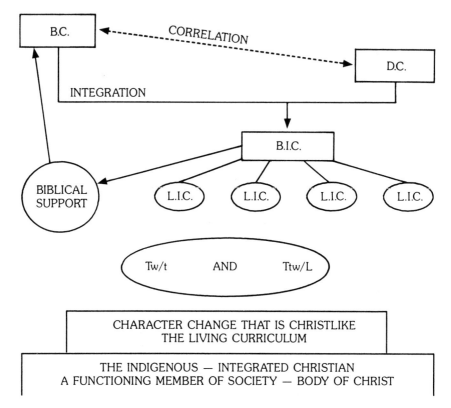

same as the rest of the animal creation that God brought into being. This statement, therefore, would either have to be rejected or modified. It is possible to say that "man is the highest form of creation" and in so doing to leave out the questionable or controversial word "animal." [See chart page 67]

At the step of correlation, though, the two truths are brought into harmony with one another and therefore complement one another. The end result in correlation is that you still have two separate concepts and have not truly achieved integration.

In the next step, the discipline concept (D.C.) and the Biblical concept (B.C.) must be brought together into a single larger expanded concept and in so doing the level of integration has been achieved. In this step, the truth from the subject area or discipline is brought together with the truth of the Word of God and in so doing we are clearly demonstrating the statement that "all truth is God's truth."

In the step of correlation, the two concepts are in harmony or complement each other but they are still two separate concepts, while in the step of integration the two concepts have been molded together into a single concept that now becomes the biblically integrated concept (B.I.C.). An additional step here would be to have the biblical support or rationale that not only gives the biblical undergirding for the biblically integrated concept, but also is the biblical framework for the concept from the Word of God (B.C.).

The next step is to take the biblically integrated concept and, at least wherever possible, begin to weave it into the life of the individual students. This is the life integrated concept (L.I.C.) and is now the step where the truth of the discipline has been woven together with the truth of the Word of God, and ultimately, this integrated concept is woven into the very life and fabric of our students.

This of course begins the lifelong process of developing character change that is Christ-like or the process of equipping students to not only be functioning members of society but also functioning members of the body of Christ. As Dr. Jim Braley would say, the teachers and the students alike become the "living curriculum" particularly at this point.

Often I am asked the question, "Where do the Character Sketches of Bill Gothard fit into this area of integration?" Actually, at the concept with concept area there really is no integration, nor for that matter even correlation. What Mr. Gothard has done is to take the abstract concept of a character trait and go to the natural realm of animal life to give to us a concrete illustration, and in so doing, has made the abstract concept much more meaningful and life related. Gothard does an excellent job of integration, not in the area of concept with concept integration, but truth with life. This is what we have always referred to as the life application step in the process of Bible study, or as Dr. Larry Richards calls it, the "took step" in the lesson. The principle from teaching and learning that applies is "the closer you stay to real life the more meaningful your teaching will be." So whenever we teach the Word of God, or for that matter any concept, to the best of our ability, we must always take that truth and meaningfully tie it to and weave it into the life of the individual student.

The Lord Jesus in His earthly teaching ministry often used the same approach. He would take an abstract biblical concept and go to a concrete natural illustration in order to make it more meaningful to his hearers. The thrust of his own teaching was clearly life application. [See chart page 66]

The question of course is, "Can every subject area (or discipline) be integrated at both the concept with concept area as well as the concept (or truth) with life area?" I am sure that some subjects are more easily integrated in the concept with concept area than others. This would especially be true if the textbook writers or the individual teacher had done a thorough job of identifying the specific mastery objectives or concepts that were to be taught. Regardless, there are two specific aspects of integration, one or both of which can always be accomplished. There is integration presuppositionally, concept with concept, the theoretical or there is integration, truth with life, the practical. [See page 16]

In the social studies discipline there is probably a greater potential for integrating truth with truth as well as truth with life. While in some disciplines,

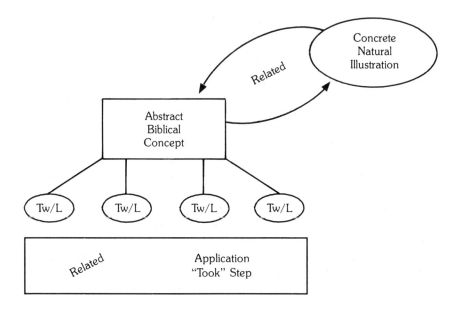

The Closer You Stay to Real Life the
More Meaningful Your
Teaching Will Be

such as math or science, it might be easier to integrate presuppositionally, concept with concept or the truth with truth aspect. In other areas, such as physical education or typing and shorthand, where the emphasis is more practical to begin with, there may be a greater degree of integration possible at the truth with life aspect. The ultimate goal in Christian education would be not only to demonstrate that all truth is God's truth (and therefore the truth from the discipline and the truth from the Word of God are capable of being woven together into a single concept), but also that all truth can be woven into the Christian world and life view of the individual student and is therefore capable of having practical application in the student's life in a meaningful way.

## Keys to the Integration Process

1. Define correlation. Answer: When two truths are in harmony with one another, complement one another, and therefore, are not in conflict with one another, there is correlation. In correlation there is the concept from the discipline complementing the biblical concept, but they remain as two separate concepts.

2. Define integration. Answer: When the concept of the discipline and the biblical concept are brought together into a single larger concept demonstrating the reality of the statement that "all truth is God's Truth," then integration has been achieved at the academic (or theoretical) aspect. When integration has been achieved, rather than having two separate concepts, a single concept emerges.

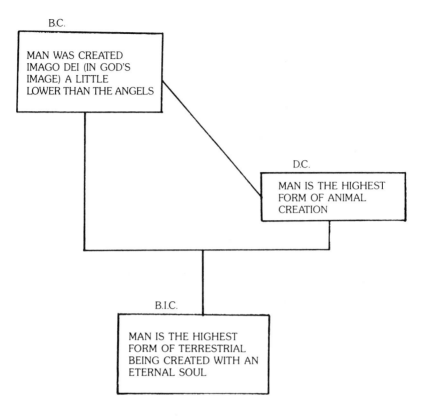

3. Explain: Truth with truth and truth with life. Answer: This occurs when the biblical concept (or the truth from the Word of God) is related to the truth (or concept) from the subject area (or discipline) in the process of academic (or theoretic) integration, and then ultimately this truth is woven into the world and life view and the real life situation of the individual student. This takes the theoretical aspect and ties it to the practical in relationship to real life.

4. What is meant by the statement "structure of the discipline"? Answer: The structure of the discipline consists of the basic principles or concepts that make up that particular discipline. This could be the basic concepts without which you would not have that particular discipline and thus it gives shape or form to the subject area.

5. What is the structure of the Bible? Answer: The structure of the Bible is formed from the basic doctrinal concepts without which you would not have the overall impact or emphasis of the Word of God. The basic doctrinal concepts would be found inductively in biblical theology rather than deductively in systematic theology. Biblical theology deals directly with the content of the Scripture, dealing with it inductively and exegetically in light of its historical (cultural) grammatical nature. Its purpose is to discern and develop the biblical concepts or principles historically from both the Old and New Testaments demonstrating the

unity of the Bible. This approach to biblical theology provides the structure of the Bible or the basic concepts, doctrines, or principles that hold all of the Scriptures together as a whole.

6. In integration, why and how is the teacher a model? Answer: The teacher becomes a model of the integrated life or of the capability of the truth of the Word of God being woven into the very fabric (or warp and woof) of an individual. As the apostle Paul states in 1 Thessalonians chapter 1, the "gospel came not unto you in word only, but also in power, and in the Holy Ghost, and in much assurance; as you know what manner of men we were among you for your sake."

7. Explain the difference between facts and concepts. Answer: A true understanding of concepts can never be had apart from seeing the meaningful relationship of the necessary facts. Concepts are facts that have been brought into meaningful relationship. Though one could have a grasp of facts, that would not necessarily preclude that he understood the concepts. Apart from seeing how the facts relate and fit together, one could never get the complete idea, the big picture, or a true understanding of the meaning of the facts.

8. What is concept-with-concept integration? Answer: When the concept from the discipline is brought together with the biblical concept into a single larger expanded concept, then we have concept with concept integration. This is the theoretical aspect of integration. The significance of this is that true integration is not taking a little fact and trying somehow to spiritualize it, but rather, it is recognizing that the two big ideas or concepts are brought together into meaningful relationship.

9. Why is contemporary awareness necessary? Answer: For the practical or real life aspect of integration to be achieved, the teacher must be able to relate meaningfully the truth not only to the life of the student, but specifically to the real life level of the student. This necessitates that the teacher not only have an adequate understanding of the truth (or concepts) but the real life of where the student actually is.

10. What is meant by the indigenous or integrated Christian? Answer: Dr. George Peters would say that an indigenous church is not only self-supporting, self-propagating, and self-governing, but also requires that the church be culturally related. He would emphasize that this cultural relatedness requires sixty to seventy percent cultural identification. In order for a church to be truly indigenous, it must have the capability of being able to relate meaningfully the gospel of faith in Christ to the contemporary culture in which it finds itself. This is what is necessary for the indigenous Christian as well. The individual believer must be able to relate meaningfully his faith in Jesus Christ (Christian world and life view) not only to the body of believers, the church, but also to the lost contemporary world. When the individual is capable of doing this, the Word of God has not only been meaningfully woven into the fabric of that individual's life, but he also has gained the capability to relate that truth meaningfully to the contemporary world.

Chapter 7

# The Concept of
# the Structure of a Discipline

What is the necessity for discovering the structure of a discipline? The concept of the structure of the discipline is concerned with the basic truth that is necessary in order to give meaning to the particular discipline. In contrast to the simple assumptions related to the particular discipline, the study of structures is more difficult and complex, but it is absolutely necessary for educators to understand this approach to curriculum development, especially in our day. If it is true that half of what students are being taught today will be obsolete in ten years and half of what they need to know in ten years has not yet been discovered, then there must be a better means of organizing the curriculum and the specifics that are being taught. Because specific facts become obsolete so rapidly, they are not significant in and of themselves. Their chief function is to explain, illustrate, or develop the main ideas or concepts. The knowledge explosion is so great that in the technical fields alone there is over four times as much technical information available today as there was at the end of the Korean War. Thus even though new facts may come to light and some of the facts may even change, the basic concepts or structures of the particular discipline remain the same.

A poem that is sometimes used in relationship to principles and methods can be adapted to illustrate this idea:

> Facts are many,
> Concepts are few;
> Facts may change,
> But concepts never do.

What then is an approximate definition of the structure of a discipline? The structure of a discipline consists of the body of concepts which define the subject matter of that discipline and helps set the parameters for further inquiries. First of all, we need to understand that there can be no true understanding of concepts apart from facts. Concepts are facts that have been brought together in a meaningful relationship. In some cases in the past it was not that the facts were necessarily wrong, but they were limited or at least lacked meaning because they were taught in the context of dogma rather than in the context of conceptions. The facts were taught as the absolutes rather than demonstrating that the facts as they related meaningfully to the larger picture really was the absolute. Facts or knowledge, especially in the scientific fields, are very fragile and subject to change and require constant research based on the updated understanding of the principles that have been accumulated.

In the successful search for more valid principles, for more adequate models to deal with the investigated knowledge, a new "shape" or character or framework has developed. Using the older approach, knowledge tended toward the shape of a catalogue. However, the present approach tends to look toward patterns, relationships and the principles to explain the particular discipline. When these patterns or concepts or structures are found, they help to shed new light on the specific items in our old catalogues.

This shift from catalogues of information to patterns or concepts in the disciplines means that teaching and learning have taken on a new dimension. Instead of focusing on one thing or idea or fact at a time, attempting to clarify each and then moving on to the next item, teaching becomes the process of focusing on points of contact, attempting to connect them together to give the big idea in order to give the larger picture or pattern that emerges.

From a Christian philosophical perspective operating on the assumption that all truth is God's truth, once the basic concepts have been discovered and tested in the light of the revealed truth of the Word of God, when these concepts are put together to form the structure of the discipline, we would have to conclude that the structure of the discipline is the same for Christian and non-Christian. Though different disciplines may have widely different conceptual structures because of the widely different questions that are asked in the inquiries and the different kinds of data they seek, we believe that there must be some means of finding common threads that would tie all of the disciplines together into a single structure. Maybe this thread or framework revolves around such concepts as independence, dependence, and interdependence. If all truth is God's truth, thus implying that all this truth is sourced in God and specifically in the person of Jesus Christ, then it would seem that there is some unifying factor that ties everything together. The Scripture tells us that all things consist or hold together in Christ (Colossians. 1:17). This is not only the nuclear glue that holds everything together, but more specifically the framework that holds all that is truth together in one Person. I indicated earlier that it was the body of concepts that gives to us the structure of the discipline. A second aspect of the structure is what could be classified as the syntax of the discipline which not only relates to how the concepts fit together to form the structure or the pattern for the particular discipline, but how these basic concepts are going to be used to attain the desired goals related to that discipline. The conceptual structure of a discipline is composed of the basic concepts or truth without which you would not have that discipline, and the difficulty is being able to state it clearly and precisely. The syntactical structure of the discipline is concerned with relationships, interrelationships and function. The significance of this for education lies precisely in the extent to which we want to teach what is true and timeless and have it understood and continue to have meaning.

How does one go about discovering the structure of a discipline? Understanding of the structure of a discipline can begin by asking the following questions:

1. What questions does it deal with?
2. What kind of questions does it seek?
3. What are the concepts it used to analyze the field?
4. What methods does it use to obtain the data?
5. How does it organize its inquiries and findings?

What are the values or benefits to be gained from approaching the subject matter from the standpoint of structure as opposed to a catalogue? First of all, the understanding of the structure of the discipline will facilitate for teachers the practical concept with concept integration. Integration is not weaving together small minute facts or bits of information, but is a matter of taking the basic concept from the discipline and seeing how it meaningfully relates to the revealed truth or the concept that is to be found within the Word of God. Secondly, it is easier to evaluate the specific concepts from the discipline in light of the truth of God's Word and thus it will be easier to discern truth and error as it may be expressed by some within the disciplines or fields of study. Thirdly, coverage of the specific content will be reduced and the depth of study hopefully increased, because now the emphasis will not be on the coverage of facts or information, but on the effective communication of concepts that have meaning. Now only the specific facts that communicate concepts will be necessary. Fourth, the learners are not now expected to remember all of the specific facts or detailed information that may have been necessary to develop an understanding of the main concept or the big idea, but retention of the concept is critical. Fifth, if teachers have an understanding of the function of the specific facts of information used in developing a concept, then they should be given the freedom to replace one set of facts with another that they feel would be more useful in communicating the concept. Sixth, the elimination of unnecessary coverage of facts and details hopefully will release time for discussion and interaction between teacher and students, thus allowing the students a greater chance to learn the process of critical thinking. Seventh, because the emphasis is no longer placed on a catalogue of facts or specific information, but on patterns or concepts, the course of study is limited to a manageable unit.

From an educational perspective at least three results can be anticipated. *First*, because the emphasis is now on the discovery of the big ideas or the concepts rather than the retention of a larger catalogue of information, it will be easier for the student to see these facts in a meaningful way as they are brought into relationships. Thus meaning or understanding should be enhanced in a conceptual or structural approach to education. The *second* result should be that there will be greater retention. Those things that are taught in isolation are much more easily lost, while those specific facts or ideas that are taught in a meaningful relationship, a structure or a concept, will be more easily retained. The principle is that the greater the degree of relatedness, the greater the degree of retention. *Thirdly*, the possibility of application, use, or function of what has been learned is much more assured than if the student had just simply been learning something for the sake of learning it and trying to remember it. From the Christian perspective the Scripture is saying to us that learning is not just for the sake of learning and remembering, but learning is for the purpose of living and a conceptual approach facilitates this.

One *final observation* can be made from the Christian perspective and that is in relationship to the approach of intergration. Approaching not only the discipline but also the Scriptures from the standpoint of the basic concept will not only enhance the potential for integrating Truth with truth, that is the biblical concept with the concept from the discipline, but the potential for being able to relate this concept meaningfully to the life of the student will also be enhanced. Thus the goal of weaving the truth of the Word of God into the concepts of the disciplines will be greatly facilitated, but also the potential for weaving the truth into the life of the student will also be enhanced.

> Facts are many,
> Concepts are few;
> Facts may change,
> But concepts never do.

Chapter 8

# An Integrated Life Studies Curriculum

## ANTHROPOLOGY

| Grade Level | Mastery Objectives |
|---|---|
| K | Understand that a person's way of life is influenced by culture and tradition. |
| 1 | Understand that likenesses and differences exist among families. |
| 2 | Understand that an individual is the product of his/her culture. Acceptance of culture enhances self-identity. |
| 3 | Understand that communities are composed of different cultures and the resulting *confluence* of cultures promotes understanding of self and others. |
| 4 | Understand that one's lifestyle today is influenced by diversity of traditions through which a culture continues to develop. |
| 5 | Understand that people identify and use resources in ways that are shaped by their culture. |
| 6 | Understand that cultures within a society may have conflicts and these often become a stimulus for social change. |

## SOCIOLOGY

| Grade Level | Mastery Objectives |
|---|---|
| K | Understand that individuals live in groups and learn from one another. |
| 1 | Understand that the family is the source of some of the most fundamental and necessary learning. |
| 2 | Understand that the personal development of an individual is affected by his social environment. |

73

**3**   Understand that one's social environment is composed of many different groups.
**4**   Understand that social behavior is learned through group interaction.
**5**   Understand that social behavior reflects and is shaped by the values of interacting groups.
**6**   Understand that every society has a system of rules, norms, values, and sanctions to guide the behavior of individuals and groups within society.

# GEOGRAPHY

**Grade Level** / **Mastery Objectives**

**K**   Understand that individuals live in different environments and adapt to those environments.
**1**   Understand that where people live influences how they live.
**2**   Understand that geographic factors influence where and how people live and what they do.
**3**   Understand that people will utilize natural resources to meet their basic needs and these resources must be protected and conserved.
**4**   Understand that the geographical features of places on the earth vary and contribute to the distinctiveness of areas.
**5**   Understand that technology helps people to utilize natural resources to meet their needs and wants.
**6**   Understand that the varying distribution of natural resources among places on the earth has led to the interdependence of peoples.

# PSYCHOLOGY

**Grade Level** / **Mastery Objectives**

**K**   Understand that each individual is unique and has worth and dignity.
**1**   Understand that all individuals possess likenesses and differences
**2**   Understand that each individual has special talents and strengths and it is possible for him to develop them.
**3**   Understand that an individual's attitudes are reflected in his/her behavior.
**4**   Understand that there are ways in which an individual can cope with his/her feelings of frustration and inadequacy.
**5**   Understand that an individual's behavior toward another is influenced by how that other individual behaves toward him/her.
**6**   Understand that an individual has control over and is responsible for his/her own behavior.

# HISTORY

| Grade Level | Mastery Objectives |
|---|---|
| K | Understand that events, traditions, and customs have roots in the past. |
| 1 | Understand that change is always occurring. |
| 2 | Understand that because change is always occurring, life in any community differs from its past. |
| 3 | Understand that change in any community is often the result of technological advancement and this change is often evident in methods of transportation, communication, and urbanization. |
| 4 | Understand that the historical past influences the present and the present cannot be adequately understood without knowledge of the past. |
| 5 | Understand that because change is always occurring, conflict may result, but differences can be resolved in different ways. |
| 6 | Understand that history demonstrates that people have been motivated by values and ideals and by material wants and needs. |

# ECONOMICS

| Grade Level | Mastery Objectives |
|---|---|
| K | Understand that a person cannot totally satisfy material wants, because the wants of humans are unlimited, whereas the resources needed to fulfill these wants are limited. |
| 1 | Understand that as a consumer, an individual must decide which needs will be met and which will not be satisfied. |
| 2 | Understand that in a work-oriented society individuals perform specialized tasks to provide goods and services for themselves and others. |
| 3 | Understand that specialization increases productivity and leads to increased interdependence among individuals and communities. |
| 4 | Understand that the patterns of buying and selling in a country or region depend on available resources and the educational and technological development of its people. |
| 5 | Understand that the patterns of buying and selling in a country or region depend on available resources and the educational and technological development of its people. |
| 6 | Understand that economic systems are shaped by the values and traditions of the culture. |

# POLITICAL SCIENCE

| Grade Level | Mastery Objectives |
| --- | --- |
| K | Understand that rules are necessary to protect the individual. |
| 1 | Understand that rules are necessary to govern the behavior of individuals within groups. |
| 2 | Understand that the members of a family are governed by a system of rules which specify positions of authority and procedures for enforcing rules. |
| 3 | Understand that the purpose of government is to protect and serve the needs of its citizens. |
| 4 | Understand that peaceful interaction within and between communities depends on a formal system of social control. |
| 5 | Understand that the pattern of government for a group of communities is determined by the degree to which the governed participate in the political system. |
| 6 | Understand that stable political organization improves the quality of life shared by its citizens. |

## SOCIAL STUDIES
### Kindergarten

**BIBLICAL CONCEPT**

As sovereign of the universe, God is in control of the circumstances that bring about culture and tradition.

**ANTHROPOLOGICAL CONCEPT**

A person's way of life is influenced by culture and tradition.

**BIBLICALLY INTEGRATED CONCEPT**

As sovereign of the universe *God still uses culture and tradition to accomplish His purposes* so that people can learn from one another.

## BACKGROUND INFORMATION FOR TEACHING THE BIC

The Bible shows how God uses culture and societies to teach people things. He used the Babylonians and their methods of warfare to purify the Jews during the exile. They returned cleansed from idolatry. God used the nation Israel and all their social customs and society to bring His Son into the world. *God used the background of Paul to prepare him for the special work which He had for him to do.* God has placed you in a special type of home to prepare you for the special life you are to live. Daniel 2:21 tells that God controls nations and their social customs. The term "fullness of time" means that God has set the whole stage for the coming of Christ. Part of that included culture.

## LEADING TO LIFE INTEGRATION
Emphasis should be placed on the things that you do with other children that help you to do God's will.
    A.  Children in your neighborhood
    B.  Children in your city
    C.  Children in other parts of the world
How did you respond or what did you do today when Bobby hit you? Bobby likes to play with cars and you like to play with a ball. Did you play cars with Bobby or did you play with a ball?

# SOCIAL STUDIES
## Grade 1

| BIBLICAL CONCEPT | ANTHROPOLOGICAL CONCEPT |
|---|---|
| God has sovereignly established the family unit. | Likenesses and differences exist among families. |

### BIBLICALLY INTEGRATED CONCEPT
God has sovereignly established the family with likenesses and differences among its members.

## BACKGROUND INFORMATION FOR TEACHING THE BIC
God established the family—Genesis 1:27, 28
God made the family a unit—Genesis 2:24
God made diversity in this unity—
    Father-Mother—Exodus 20:12, Deuteronomy 5:16
    Brothers and sisters—Genesis 4:2, 20:12
    Aunts, uncles, cousins—Leviticus 10:4, Numbers 36:11, 1 Samuel 14:50
God gave each various responsibilities
    Father—Genesis 50:16, Proverbs 1:8, Genesis 37:10, Genesis 25:28
    Mother—Genesis 25:23, Proverbs 4:3, 30
    Children—Psalm 127:3-5, Exodus 20:12

## LEADING TO LIFE INTEGRATION
Emphasis should be placed on the following:
    A.  Makeup of the Family

B. Likenesses and Differences in Family
   1. Age
   2. Sex
   3. Responsibility

# SOCIAL STUDIES
## Grade 2

### BIBLICAL CONCEPT
God is in sovereign control of all forces to accomplish ultimate good.

### ANTHROPOLOGICAL CONCEPT
An individual is the product of his/her culture. Acceptance of culture enhances self-identity.

### BIBLICALLY INTEGRATED CONCEPT
One's self-concept is *enhanced* to the degree that he/she recognizes God's use of culture to accomplish ultimate good in his/her life.

## BACKGROUND INFORMATION FOR TEACHING THE BIC
For the believer acceptance should be on the basis of God's acceptance of us.
   Ephesians 2:10—For we are his workmanship, created in Christ Jesus unto good works, which God hath before ordained that we should walk in them.
   Romans 9:20-22—Potter and clay
   Psalm 129:14-16—I will praise thee, for I am wonderfully made. God has made each of us who we are. God has put us in the home and the school we are in for a reason. God is working in our lives daily to make us what he wants us to be.
   2 Corinthians 12:7-10—Paul's thorn, "Therefore I take pleasure in infirmities, in reproaches, in necessities, in persecutions, in distress for Christ's sake, for when I am weak, then am I strong."
   Romans 8:28—"And we know that all things work together for good to them that love God, to them who are the called according to his purpose."
   Philippians 4:11—I have learned to be content (book is full of joy).

## LEADING TO LIFE INTEGRATION
Illustrations:
   Paul—raised a devout Jew; was used to reach the Jewish people.

Timothy—Father a Greek; mother and grandmother taught him.
Joseph—hard circumstances worked to his good.

# SOCIAL STUDIES
## Grade 3

### BIBLICAL CONCEPT

God sovereignly created man with a unique personality and purpose and scattered him throughout the world.

### ANTHROPOLOGICAL CONCEPT

Communities are composed of different cultures and the resulting *confluence* of cultures promotes understanding of self and others.

### BIBLICALLY INTEGRATED CONCEPT

God sovereignly created man with a unique personality and purpose and has permitted a confluence of cultures to develop. An awareness of God's perspective and an understanding of His purpose enhances one's understanding of self and others which enables him/her to function better in society.

## BACKGROUND INFORMATION FOR TEACHING THE BIC
Genesis 1—Creation (in the image of God).
Hebrews 2:6-8—Man is created as a vital responsible part of creation.
Genesis 11—Tower of Babel (differing cultures began).
Concept of Jewish proselyting (no favorites with God).
Acts 2:5-12—People from all cultures hear the gospel.
Leviticus—Instructions in development of Jewish culture.
Revelations 20:11-12—People from all cultures stand before the same God.
John 4—Jesus supercedes cultural boundaries (Samaritan Woman).

## LEADING TO LIFE INTEGRATION
Emphasis should be placed upon relationships between groups such as:
A. Natural
B. Economic
C. Educational
D. Religious

# SOCIAL STUDIES
## Grade 4

### BIBLICAL CONCEPT

The principles of God's Word are supra-cultural and are always applicable regardless of the diversity of traditions and the development of culture.

### ANTHROPOLOGICAL CONCEPT

One's lifestyle today is influenced by diversity of traditions through which a culture continues to develop.

### BIBLICALLY INTEGRATED CONCEPT

The lifestyle of the Christian community (church) should so positively influence the culture that the culture begins to reflect the absolute principles of God's Word. Though it is not probable that a single individual will bring about cultural change, a corporate body could easily have great influence.

### BACKGROUND INFORMATION FOR TEACHING THE BIC

The message of Jesus found in Matthew 5:13-16, Mark 9:50, Luke 14:34, and John 13:34-35 shows the believer's responsibility to influence his world. The Christian is to be salt and light in his community. God used the lives of His children to testify of Himself.

Each of these imperatives were given to a group of people, not an individual.

### LEADING TO LIFE INTEGRATION

Emphasis should be placed on developing a Christian lifestyle in relationship to these areas:

A. Culture
B. Traditions
C. Education
D. Values

It is possible to maintain biblical absolutism as well as cultural relatedness (life relatedness) or biblical contextualization.

# SOCIAL STUDIES
## Grade 5

### BIBLICAL CONCEPT

All the resources of the universe exist because of the creative act of God.

### ANTHROPOLOGICAL CONCEPT

People identify and use resources in ways that are shaped by their culture.

### BIBLICALLY INTEGRATED CONCEPT

The sovereign Creator has charged man with the responsible use of the universe's resources within the context of contemporary cultural influence.

### BACKGROUND INFORMATION FOR TEACHING THE BIC

Adam was given the responsibility of subduing the earth and the privilege of taking from it only what he needed for the sustenance of life (Genesis 1:27-29). However, because of man's fallen nature, man has refused to recognize this fact and has determined to extract as much as possible from the land — whatever his culture demands (Romans 1:20, 21, 29-32).

### LEADING TO LIFE INTEGRATION

Define customs and traditions. What customs and traditions do we have in our culture? Which ones can affect the environment? How can we modify them or change them to protect the environment? For example, the annual Christmas tree is usually cut down. How long does it take that tree to grow? Think of some alternatives:

1. Decorate a permanent tree in the front yard—no tree in the house.
2. Plant a small pine in pot for indoors. After Christmas, plant it as a windbreak, adding to it each year.

Define needs. List the resources we need for survival.

Food—plant a garden. Mothers "recycle" food through leftovers. Plan a balanced menu to show the foods we require.

Chemicals—What is the difference between organic and chemical fertilizer? How do chemicals affect the environment?

Define wants. List what we often want in our lives. What wants affect the environment? For example, the temperature at home is set at 72 degrees when it can be set at 68; wise use of gas and oil resources.

Define value systems. From the definition, what two value systems exist in the world?

God's—Matthew 6:19-21; 16:24-34.

Man's—Romans 1:20, 21, 29-32.

Considering the value system a Christian should have, how does it affect our use of the resources in our world, our customs and traditions, our needs and our wants?

Point out that without a specific biblical reason behind our motives, conservation and preservation become simply a good way to live.

# SOCIAL STUDIES

## Grade 6

| BIBLICAL CONCEPT | ANTHROPOLOGICAL CONCEPT |
|---|---|
| The supra-cultural principles of God's Word are consistent and determinative and never change. | Cultures within a society may have conflicts and these often become a stimulus for social change. |

### BIBLICALLY INTEGRATED CONCEPT

The supra-cultural principles of God's Word are the stimuli and evaluative criteria for social change, and though society constantly changes, the absolutes of His Word never change. Thus all changes in society must be viewed through the Word of God.

### BACKGROUND INFORMATION FOR TEACHING THE BIC

For the teacher:

Cultures within a society may interact either in cooperation or conflict, either of which may be a stimulus for social change.

The supra-cultural principles of God's Word are consistent, determinative, and applicable to any people or time. God's principles are not bound by culture.

The supra-cultural principles of God's Word are the evaluative and directive criteria for the social change which may result from the cooperation or conflict that occurs between cultures within one society.

## LEADING TO LIFE INTEGRATION
Emphasis should be placed on the fact that conflict leads to social change in these areas:

Human rights
Race relations
Religious affiliations
Political parties/factions
Marriage/family
Authority structures
Status & role of men and women
Social class structures
Individual autonomy vs. group dependence/control

# SOCIAL STUDIES

## Kindergarten

### BIBLICAL CONCEPT
God knew that it was not good for man to be alone.

### SOCIOLOGICAL CONCEPT
Individuals live in groups and learn from one another.

### BIBLICALLY INTEGRATED CONCEPT
God has organized life in such a way that people live in groups in order to learn from and help one another.

## BACKGROUND INFORMATION FOR TEACHING BIC
Genesis 2:18-24 gives us the institution of the home and family with God's commentary that "it is not good that the man should be alone." The New Testament concept of "one another" should also be studied.

## LEADING TO LIFE INTEGRATION
Emphasis should be placed on the family and developing strong interpersonal relationships.

We must learn to obey parents.
We must get along well with brothers and sisters.
Child must learn to obey authorities in school.
Children must help each other in school.
We must treat others as we want to be treated.

# SOCIAL STUDIES
## Grade 1

**BIBLICAL CONCEPT**

God has sovereignly established the family as the fundamental unit of society.

**SOCIOLOGICAL CONCEPT**

The family is the source of some of the most fundamental and necessary learning.

### BIBLICALLY INTEGRATED CONCEPT

God has sovereignly established the family as the fundamental center of learning.

### BACKGROUND INFORMATION FOR TEACHING THE BIC

According to Deuteronomy 4:9-10, the responsibility of learning about God belongs to the father and broadly the parents. That which is to be taught is not only an academic abstract truth but that truth which the parent has experienced taught by God Himself. The father is to remember these things so that he will not depart from God, and he is also to teach these truths to his children so that they will come to know, and not depart from following after God.

In Deuteronomy 11:19-20 the time of instruction, manner and methods are implied. All time is to be used for instruction, in a constant and continual teaching that the heart forgets not.

### LEADING TO LIFE INTEGRATION

Emphasis should be placed on the purpose of the family, the structure of the family, and the essentials for a happy home.

# SOCIAL STUDIES
## Grade 2

**BIBLICAL CONCEPT**

The principles of God's Word provides guidance and direction for one's personal development, physically, mentally, emotionally, socially and spiritually.

**SOCIOLOGICAL CONCEPT**

The personal development of an individual is affected by his social environment.

### BIBLICALLY INTEGRATED CONCEPT

The personal development of individual Christians, while influenced by social environment, must

always be under the guidance and
direction of the principles of God's
Word and the Holy Spirit's super-
natural control and enablement.

## BACKGROUND INFORMATION FOR TEACHING THE BIC
Key principles in God's Word:
Love one another (positively)
Ten Commandments (some negative)
Personal biblical examples showing God's character.
Christian Ethics

## LEADING TO LIFE INTEGRATION
Emphasis should be placed on the following concepts:
Ethnic characteristics
Customs
Traditions
Art
Literature
Entertainment (recreation/leisure)

Basic principles such as the commandments never change and therefore they remain a guide for all generations, both in the matter of positives and negatives.

1. Ethnic Character — Give positive classroom exposure to any who might be different from the majority. This might be having a student in the classroom be a leader, invite adults to present information about their country (missionaries might do the same), make use of stories about other peoples and other lands. At the second grade level you could probably promote this by giving information about other groups and showing acceptance of them. Children cannot love those they do not know. Teachers could read stories of other lands and people in the storytime.

2. Customs — Customs are a part of the ethnic character of a people. Therefore, what is done to inform the student about ethnic differences will also highlight culture. Many of the concepts shared by those who might visit the class, or stories that might be read by the teacher, will highlight the customs of a culture.

It might also be interesting to investigate some of the cultural customs of the Hebrew people in the Old Testament, or some of the groups represented in the New Testament.

During this time of learning, customs emphasized in the different homes represented in the class may be discussed. Teachers must be careful not to undermine parents and their customs.

3. Art — The arts of different people are varied. Here is a good opportunity to share some of the culturally different art forms, crafts, and designs from many different peoples and cultures.

4. Literature — The literature of any people tells a great deal about their ethnic character and their customs. It would be interesting to read some stories from other cultures which highlight wholesome differences. A good selection of stories from many lands could be acquired at most libraries.

5. Entertainment (recreation/leisure) — What different cultures do for entertainment is very interesting. A study of some of the children's games which come from different lands would be of interest. This information is readily available in most encyclopedias. Cover the wide expanse of the many different things which can be done for entertainment, recreation or leisure. It will take some work to avoid talking only of movies, television, and professional sports. Children need to see the many differing entertainments used by different cultures, and how to make best use of entertainment, recreation and leisure in their own lives from a biblical perspective.

# SOCIAL STUDIES
## Grade 3

### BIBLICAL CONCEPT
God has created man as a social being with the capacity for developing relationships.

### SOCIOLOGICAL CONCEPT
One's social environment is composed of many different groups.

### BIBLICALLY INTEGRATED CONCEPT
The purposes of God in the social environment are realized through interaction with a variety of different groups and with God Himself.

### BACKGROUND INFORMATION FOR TEACHING BIC
The basic idea to communicate is that God is the author of the structure of society and that His will is accomplished by more than one kind of person.

A good place to begin might be the story of the tower of Babel where God told the people to spread out and multiply. When they refused to do so, God instituted different languages so the people would have to scatter and multiply. Thus we have God stepping into history and forming groups which led to the broad diversification of culture that we see around us in the world today.

### LEADING TO LIFE INTEGRATION
The culture of Israel in the time of David and Solomon could be explained to illustrate how the various social groups functioned and contributed to the smooth operation of a country.

Concepts such as "environment" and "capacity" will need explanation.

# SOCIAL STUDIES
## Grade 4

### BIBLICAL CONCEPT
The achievement of God's purposes necessitates group structure and relationships intending for us to work together in unity.

### SOCIOLOGICAL CONCEPT
Social behavior is learned through group interaction.

### BIBLICALLY INTEGRATED CONCEPT
The purposes of God can be realized in one's social environment as men function in meaningful interrelationships.

### BACKGROUND INFORMATION FOR TEACHING THE BIC
Ephesians 1:22, 23—We are members of what is called the body of Christ. This is the church. It is a group of people who all work together—worship, learn and teach.

Ephesians 6:1-4—We are a part of a family group. God planned it this way and we are to obey our parents.

Matthew 16:18 (the church); Romans 12:4, 5; 1 Corinthians 12:12-27; Ephesians 4:16.

### LEADING TO LIFE INTEGRATION
Learning responsible behavior
Types of responsibility to those in authority
Factors that determine responsibility

| OBEDIENCE TO AUTHORITIES | TYPES | FACTORS |
|---|---|---|
| Parents | Obedience | Volunteering |
| Teachers | Respect | Helpfulness |
| Principal | Compassion | Unselfishness |
| Pastor | Volunteering | |

# SOCIAL STUDIES
## Grade 5

### BIBLICAL CONCEPT
The achievement of God's purposes necessitates group structure and interaction.

### SOCIOLOGICAL CONCEPT
Social behavior reflects and is shaped by the values of interacting groups.

### BIBLICALLY INTEGRATED
### CONCEPT
The purposes of God are realized in the social environment as men function in meaningful interrelationships guided by the Holy Spirit and biblical values dealing with interpersonal relationships.

## BACKGROUND INFORMATION FOR TEACHING THE BIC
An excellent example of this is found in the teaching of Jesus in the parable of the Good Samaritan in Luke 10:25-37. The lawyer was going to love God and love his neighbor on his own terms and within his own system. Jesus reversed the emphasis of "Who is my neighbor?" to "Are you a neighbor?" A man shows that he has eternal life by acting for the benefit of the person in need.

An expansion of this would be the concept of the body of Christ in the Epistles. First Corinthians 12 shows the interrelationship of each individual to the whole. Members are to have the same care one for another. Ephesians 4:12 shows how various individuals are gifted and given to prepare the people of God for works of service, so that the body of Christ might be built up. The very next verse relates this to God's purpose of maturation into the perfection in Christ. Therefore, the concept is biblical in its basis.

The best teaching dealing with the concept of interrelationships is found in Jesus' teaching of forgiveness in Luke 17:3, 4.

> Verse 3—"Take heed to yourselves; If thy brother trespass against thee, rebuke him: and if he repent, forgive him."

> Verse 4—"And if he trespass against thee seven times in a day turn again to thee saying, I repent: thou shalt forgive him."

## LEADING TO LIFE INTEGRATION
This best describes how Christ shows us how interpersonal relations grow through an interrelationship achieving God's purpose. Grace to our peers is an outgrowth of salvation in Christ.

| **BIBLICAL CONCEPT** | **SOCIOLOGICAL CONCEPT** |
|---|---|
| Love God and love neighbor | Human beings need to be shown love |

### BIBLICALLY INTEGRATED
### CONCEPT
Our love must be vertical and horizontal. We cannot possess one without the other. It only makes sense that if we love God, we will love His creation.

## BACKGROUND INFORMATION FOR TEACHING THE BIC
Matthew 25:44 and 1 John 3:17—In the way we treat others, we treat Christ.

## LEADING TO LIFE INTEGRATION
It's one thing to *see* a need; it's another thing to *act*. Illustration: If you are very sick, wouldn't you want someone to visit you?

A fifth grader may understand the body concept if an athletic illustration is used. Example: A four-man basketball team is at a far greater disadvantage than a five-man team.

# SOCIAL STUDIES
## Grade 6

### BIBLICAL CONCEPT
The Bible stands as the final authority to guide and evaluate behavior.

### SOCIOLOGICAL CONCEPT
Every society has a system of rules, norms, values, and sanctions to guide the behavior of individuals and groups within society.

### BIBLICALLY INTEGRATED CONCEPT
The Bible provides for every society the final authority to guide and evaluate the behavior of individuals and of groups within that society.

## BACKGROUND INFORMATION FOR TEACHING THE BIC
The Bible deals with principles concerning man including all mankind in Adam. (Genesis 2:3, Romans 3:23, Isaiah 55)

The Bible is true, authoritative, inspired, inerrant, infallible in the original autographs. Therefore it is the final authority and message from God. (2 Timothy 3:16, 17; 1 Peter 1:21; and Psalm 119:19) Moses, the prophets, Jesus and the Apostles all based their lives on this revelation of God.

The Holy Spirit used the Word to guide and evaluate behavior of individuals and groups. (Hebrews 4:12; Psalm 119:9, 11; John 15:7; 1 Timothy 3:16, 17) We are to obey God's Word. Nations are to obey God's Word.

## LEADING TO LIFE INTEGRATION
Emphasis should be placed on the following within a given society:
Rules
Norms
Values
Sanctions

# SOCIAL STUDIES
## Kindergarten

| BIBLICAL CONCEPT | GEOGRAPHICAL CONCEPT |
|---|---|
| Both environment and man were created by God, with man having the capacity to adapt to the environment. | Understand that individuals live in different environments and adapt to those environments. |

### BIBLICALLY INTEGRATED CONCEPT
God created the earth with great geographical variety and placed in it man who has been endowed with a great capacity to adapt.

### BACKGROUND INFORMATION FOR TEACHING THE BIC
Explanation: God designed and created man a spiritual and rational being with a body and He also created a corresponding physical habitat. It was his pleasure to make the earth with a great variety of climates and resources. At the same time man possesses psychological faculties to live and prosper in any except the most extreme geographical situations. The basic provisions for physical survival can be found wherever man can go by natural means.

God has given man the ability in resources and tools to adjust and live in a diversity of geographical situations. Noah (Genesis 6) is an example of this.

### LEADING TO LIFE INTEGRATION
Locate a missionary that works and lives in a different environment. Have him visit and explain his own adaptation to a new environment.

Take advantage of the interest in the moon to show how much more beautiful God has created this world for our survival and enjoyment.

Take the class on nature walks, explaining (or at least drawing attention to) changes in the plant and animal life to adapt to changes of seasons and physical conditions.

# SOCIAL STUDIES
## Grade 1

| BIBLICAL CONCEPT | GEOGRAPHICAL CONCEPT |
|---|---|
| God made man dependent on but not totally determined by, his surroundings. | Where people live influences how they live. |

## BIBLICALLY INTEGRATED CONCEPT

God established a relationship so that man is not completely free in the way he lives, but is dependent on local conditions.

## BACKGROUND INFORMATION FOR TEACHING THE BIC

The Cost of Eden - Genesis 1-3 (location 2:8-14.)

Blessed features illustrated before failure. Divine supplies as stated in Genesis 2:15-16, the gift of marriage 2:23-25, but the key is in 1:26-31, *man's dominion*. His dependence upon his surroundings (2:16) also illustrated in the exclusion (3:22-24). After the Fall we note the surroundings have changed but man's dependence upon his surroundings has not changed. (Illustrated in Genesis 3:17-19, 23)

# SOCIAL STUDIES
## Grade 2

### BIBLICAL CONCEPT

God created man with the freedom and the ability to make purposeful choices within natural limits.

### GEOGRAPHICAL CONCEPT

Geographic factors influence where and how people live and what they do.

## BIBLICALLY INTEGRATED CONCEPT

God has made man with the ability to choose within natural limits the place, the corresponding life style and purposeful activities.

## BACKGROUND INFORMATION FOR TEACHING THE BIC

Conditions of living range from optimal to minimal depending on geographical factors. God intended man to use his mental faculties to make choices with the limits of these factors regarding the place and way of living. God also gave man the desire to engage in meaningful activities that lead to the fulfillment of his potential. Man therefore will adjust to the local geographical conditions or move to other environments.

## LEADING TO LIFE INTEGRATION

1. Ask the children where they live in the city.
   a. Cite resources such as stores and libraries close to home.
   b. Survey other areas students have lived in and cite resources of those cities.

# SOCIAL STUDIES
## Grade 3

**BIBLICAL CONCEPT**

God has given man the ability to use and care for the earth.

**GEOGRAPHICAL CONCEPT**

People will utilize natural resources to meet their basic needs and these resources must be protected and conserved.

### BIBLICALLY INTEGRATED CONCEPT

God has given man the ability to use natural resources to meet his physical needs and the responsibility to wisely use and care for resources.

## BACKGROUND INFORMATION FOR TEACHING THE BIC

Genesis 1:28-30—Man has been given dominion over the earth to use and subdue it.

## LEADING TO LIFE INTEGRATION

The student must understand the relationship between God and the world, God and man, and man and the world (1 John 1:7). The vertical fellowship with God will produce the horizontal fellowship with our brothers and sisters in the Body of Christ (one another). See list of "one anothers" from the Scripture.

### ONE ANOTHER

1. Live at peace with one another. Mark 9:50
2. Wash the feet of one another. John 13:14
3. Love one another. John 13:34-35; 15:12, 17; Romans 13:8; 1 Thessalonians 3:12; 4:9; 2 Thessalonians 1:3; 1 Peter 1:22; 1 John 3:11, 23; 4:7, 11, 12; 2 John 5
4. We are members of one another. Romans 12:5
5. Be devoted to one another in brotherly love. Romans 12:10
6. Esteem one another more highly with honor. Romans 12:10
7. Be of the same mind toward one another. Romans 12:16; 15:5
8. No longer judge one another. Romans 14:13
9. Pursue the things that provide edification for one another. Romans 14:19
10. Receive one another. Romans 15:7
11. Admonish one another. Romans 15:14
12. Greet one another with a holy kiss. Romans 16:16; 1 Corinthians 16:20; 2 Corinthians 13:12; 1 Peter 5:14
13. Do not defraud one another. 1 Corinthians 7:5

14. Wait for one another. 1 Corinthians 11:33
15. Worry about one another. 1 Corinthians 12:25
16. Be slaves to one another. Galatians 5:13
17. Don't bite and devour one another. Galatians 5:15
18. Stop challenging one another. Galatians 5:26
19. Stop envying one another. Galatians 5:26
20. Bear one another's burdens. Galatians 6:2
21. Put up with one another. Ephesians 4:2; Colossians 3:13
22. We are members of one another. Ephesians 4:24
23. Be kind toward one another. Ephesians 4:32
24. Submit yourselves to one another. Ephesians 5:21
25. Regard one another as better than yourselves. Philippians 2:3
26. Stop lying against one another. Colossians 3:9
27. Comfort one another. 1 Thessalonians 4:18; 5:11
28. Pursue good toward one another. 1 Thessalonians 5:15
29. Stir up one another to love and good works. Hebrews 10:24
30. Stop speaking against one another. James 4:11
31. Stop complaining against one another. James 5:9
32. Confess your sins to one another. James 5:16
33. Pray for one another. James 5:16
34. Show hospitality to one another. 1 Peter 4:9
35. Show humility to one another. 1 Peter 5:5

# SOCIAL STUDIES

## Grade 4

### BIBLICAL CONCEPT

God has made the earth to reflect His vast and marvelous creative ability.

### GEOGRAPHICAL CONCEPT

The geographical features of places on the earth vary and contribute to the distinctiveness of areas.

### BIBLICALLY INTEGRATED CONCEPT

God has created the earth with variety and each place has its own characteristics which reveal the great power of God.

### BACKGROUND INFORMATION FOR TEACHING THE BIC

The biblical support is widespread in the Word. For example:

Psalm 19:1—"The heavens declare the glory of God and the firmament showeth His handiwork."

Isaiah 20:12—"Who has measured the waters in the hollow of his hand, or with the breadth of his hand harked off the heavens? Who has held the dust of the earth in a basket, or weighed the mountains on the scales and the hills in a balance?"

Genesis 1:1—"In the beginning God created the heavens and the earth."

Genesis 1:31—"God saw all that He had made and it was very good."

# SOCIAL STUDIES
## Grade 5

### BIBLICAL CONCEPT
God has created man with rational ability and created the natural resources of the universe.

### GEOGRAPHICAL CONCEPT
Technology helps people to utilize natural resources to meet their needs and wants.

### BIBLICALLY INTEGRATED CONCEPT
God has created man with rational capabilities to utilize through technology the natural resources to meet his needs.

### BACKGROUND INFORMATION FOR TEACHING THE BIC

God created man in His own image (Genesis 1:26, 27) and gave him dominion over all the earth. He was to subdue the earth (Genesis 1:28). Furthermore, God gave man the mind to use the earth. God brought all the animals of the earth to Adam for him to name (Genesis 2:20), a task for the most intelligent of men. Furthermore, God made man a rational creature able to make choices. God used man's construction technology to provide Noah's ark. God gave Noah the plans and Noah followed them. God also specifically gave man dominion over the animals and plants in Genesis 1:30. Lastly the very fact that God held Adam accountable for his actions proves that He saw Adam as a rational being, capable of making his own decisions and liable for them (Genesis 3:17-19, 23).

### LEADING TO LIFE INTEGRATION

God has given man the responsibility to use his knowledge to meet the needs of all mankind, not just our nation. He has not given us this ability so that we can spend all our time and resources searching for ways to destroy ourselves through advanced weaponry. Man should use his technological advantages to meet such problems as starvation, disease, overpopulation and crime. Christians should use all the technology at their disposal to bring men to a saving knowledge of God's Word and His plan of salvation for them.

# SOCIAL STUDIES
## Grade 6

### BIBLICAL CONCEPT
God is in control of the resources and their distribution to make people (the nations) aware that they are not self-sufficient.

### GEOGRAPHICAL CONCEPT
The varying distribution of natural resources among places on the earth has led to the interdependence of peoples.

### BIBLICALLY INTEGRATED CONCEPT
God controls the wealth of the nations and carries out this purpose by interdependence between them through an uneven distribution of natural resources.

## BACKGROUND INFORMATION FOR TEACHING THE BIC
God designed the uneven distribution of the earth's natural goods to teach man that his dependence is of Him. Since God often uses a man, a group of men, and sometimes whole nations to meet the needs of other people, He has used this varying distribution of natural resources as an educational means towards teaching man to develop friendly relationships between the differing segments of the human race.

With growing population and expanding technology, some national resources are exhaused rapidly and must be supplemented with products found elsewhere. This forces nations to material interdependence and trade. In the hands of sinful man, this dependence has been used as a weapon in conflicts which will increase in the end time as predicted by God (Matthew 24:5-14; 2 Timothy 3:1-5; 2 Peter 2:9-12). This dependence has also been misused by stronger nations to deplete the resources of weaker ones, thereby suppressing them and making them even poorer than before.

Psalm 104 illustrates this very well. The waters went to the place where God assigned them (vv. 6-10) to give water to the beasts of the field, the wild donkeys, and the birds (vv. 11, 12). The waters also satisfied the earth, made the grass grow for the cattle and plants for food for man (vv. 13-15).

God made all the earth, and all the creatures in it and they all look to Him for food (vv. 24-29). (Also see Haggai 1:3-11; Matthew 6:11, 25-34; Philippians 4:19; Genesis 1; Psalm 95:3-7; 100:1-3; 102:25; I Chronicles 29:10-12.)

## LEADING TO LIFE INTEGRATION
Homework: Bring in "current events" from the newspaper having to do with foreign countries and their abundance of resources.

- Make a list of neighboring countries with resources vital to U.S.
- Make additional lists of states of America with their resources, e.g. Pennsylvania: coal, lumber.

Question/Answer time:
- Why does man need friendships?
- Why does it seem so difficult for man to form friendships?
- What type of relationship does the U.S. have with other countries?
- Because of the lack of friendship, what effect does it have upon the people, resources, and prices?
- Can you think of a story in which you had something that your friend wanted or needed? What was your reaction? What did you do?

# SOCIAL STUDIES

## Kindergarten

### BIBLICAL CONCEPT
God created man in His image.

### PSYCHOLOGICAL CONCEPT
Each individual is unique and has worth and dignity.

### BIBLICALLY INTEGRATED CONCEPT
God has uniquely made each person and each person has the potential for eternal worth and dignity through a personal relationship with Christ.

### BACKGROUND INFORMATION FOR TEACHING THE BIC
Psalm 139:14 says "I will praise thee for I am fearfully and wonderfully made. Marvelous are thy works, and that my soul knoweth right well." We are unique individuals made with the *potential* for eternal worth-life. John 3:36, "He that believeth on the Son hath everlasting life; and he that believeth not the Son shall not see life. . . . " 1 Corinthians 3:13, "Every man's work shall be made manifest; for the day shall declare it, because it shall be revealed by fire; and the fire shall test every man's work of what sort it is!"

Genesis 1:27—"So God created man in his own image, in the image of God created he him; male and female created he them."

Isaiah 43:1—"But now thus saith the Lord who created Thee, O Jacob, and he who formed Thee O Israel, Fear not; for I have redeemed Thee, I have called Thee by Thy name; Thou art mine."

# SOCIAL STUDIES
## Grade 1

**BIBLICAL CONCEPT**
God has sovereignly created man as an individual personality.

**PSYCHOLOGICAL CONCEPT**
All individuals possess likenesses and differences.

**BIBLICALLY INTEGRATED CONCEPT**
God has sovereignly created man as an individual personality possessing likenesses and differences.

### BACKGROUND INFORMATION FOR TEACHING THE BIC
Psalm 139:14-16—The Psalmist declares that all of God's works are wonderful but distinguishes man with the added description of being "fearfully and wonderfully made." Man is not something put together by accident, but is the result of God's perfect plan and will, being formed and purposed by God long before birth. Man must be of great value to God.
Genesis 5:1, 2

### LEADING TO LIFE INTEGRATION
1. Man is no accident of evolution but the product of God created in His own image. God did not create haphazardly.

2. God has created man as a unique individual. No two people are identical. Therefore, I should not try to be like someone else. That is saying that God did a poor job.

3. Luke 1:18; Jeremiah 1:4, 5; Genesis 25:21-23; Matthew 1:18—"Before I formed thee in the womb, I knew thee." Look for the positive qualities that God put in your life and others.

# SOCIAL STUDIES
## Grade 2

**BIBLICAL CONCEPT**
God's grace has endowed all men with talents and abilities.

**PSYCHOLOGICAL CONCEPT**
Each individual has special talents and strengths and it is possible for him to develop them.

### BIBLICALLY INTEGRATED
### CONCEPT

God's common grace has endowed all men (Genesis 39:5; Psalm
145:9) with certain talents and
abilities and His special grace
equips the believer for ministry
(Romans 12:3-13, especially
verse 7), and it is possible to
develop both of these areas.

## BACKGROUND INFORMATION FOR TEACHING THE BIC

God's common grace is clearly seen for example in the various fields of
science; in medicine we see men who have different abilities. Some are capable
of doing research, others are talented for surgery, or other areas of specialty
(neurological, etc.). God's grace and mercy endows these talents and abilities
to men for the preservation and blessing of His creation and His people. We
need to develop our special talents and/or abilities. It is important to recognize
needs and develop helping attitudes.

# SOCIAL STUDIES
# Grade 3

### BIBLICAL CONCEPT

God's perspective states that as a
man thinks in his heart so is he.

### PSYCHOLOGICAL CONCEPT

An individual's attitudes are reflected in his/her behavior.

### BIBLICALLY INTEGRATED
### CONCEPT

An individual's godly or ungodly
thinking and attitudes are reflected
in his/her behavior.

## BACKGROUND INFORMATION FOR TEACHING THE BIC

The following values need to be developed with an emphasis on personal
responsibility.

Values in a Community Regarding:

A. Human Rights
B. Work Ethic
C. Morality

D. Economics
E. Spiritual Development

Hebrews 11 - Faith
James 1:26 - Works
James 2:19-23 - Works
David - Bathsheba - Problem (2 Samuel 10-12); Process (Psalm 51).
Ananias and Sapphira - Lying (Acts 5:1-11); Position (Psalm 32).
Demas - Forsaken Paul (2 Timothy 4:10)
Romans 7:15-25 - that which I do! The inner struggle.

# SOCIAL STUDIES
## Grade 4

### BIBLICAL CONCEPT
God supernaturally provides the resources needed to cope with feelings of frustration and inadequacy.

### PSYCHOLOGICAL CONCEPT
There are ways in which an individual can cope with his/her feelings of frustration and inadequacy.

### BIBLICALLY INTEGRATED CONCEPT
God through His Word and the ministry of the Holy Spirit enables the Christian to cope with personal feelings of frustration and inadequacy.

### BACKGROUND INFORMATION FOR TEACHING THE BIC
Genesis 17:19—Abraham's frustration over not having a son was countered by the promise of God.

Galatians 5:22-23—Through the ministry of the Holy Spirit a believer does not have to "blow up" when he is frustrated. The Holy Spirit gives the believer self-control.

1 Corinthians 10:13—When we are being tempted we have the assurance that God will provide a way for us so that we can stand up under the pressure.

### LEADING TO LIFE INTEGRATION
Example of a child having feelings of frustration and inadequacy concerning schoolwork.

1. Teach them that all boys and girls are a very special creation of God. God considered Adam and Eve and all the rest of creation as "very good."

God has a special relationship with his and special plan for his life. He should have a "good feeling" about himself. His schoolwork helps him to learn more about God, himself, other people, life, and what God has in store for him.

2. However, Adam and Eve didn't obey God and it hurt their relationship with Him. It was their fault, not God's. Every one of us has done the same thing. We are not the same as God originally made us. We cannot do things as well as we could. Now we get mad and angry at God and ourselves when we can't do everything right. Adam and Eve probably felt frustration and inadequacy after they disobeyed God. When they did things, it was harder than it was before.

3. It is not uncommon for boys and girls to experience this kind of feeling. No student is "odd" or "stupid" because he is having trouble with his schoolwork. Everyone had the kind of feelings he has at some time. (His problems and feelings are real and should not be denied.)

4. However, God has made a way for us to do well in our schoolwork no matter how "smart" we are! We do not have to feel like we can't do it. We do not have to feel we are not as good as the other boys and girls in class.

5. Statement, "Do you know that if we ask God to forgive us for disobeying Him, He will forgive us, love us and forget all about what we did?"

"Do you know that if we ask God to forgive us for getting angry and giving up when we do our schoolwork, He promises to help us Himself? Just think of God helping us with our schoolwork. We don't have to get mad or say we can't do it when we have problems." (Make it a point that there still will be difficulties.)—Genesis 17:19.

6. God wants to teach us about many, many things when we go to school. When we ask Jesus to forgive us and help us as a friend at school, His Holy Spirit is always present to help us. He helps us to listen to the teacher very closely, to behave, and not to give up when we get angry and say "I can't do it!" When God promises to help us, He will never give up on us no matter how hard of a time we have with our schoolwork—Galatians 5:22-23.

7. When school gets so hard that I want to give up, I have to remember that God is still with me and that the Holy Spirit is right by my side! As long as I do my very best and work hard and don't give up, it doesn't matter if I don't do as well as the rest of the class. I know that God still loves me and that He is teaching me something very special and making me a better person. As long as I obey in class, and do all the work the teacher gives me, and believe the Holy Spirit will help me to do my best, it doesn't matter what grade I get, God will still give me an "A!"—1 Corinthians 10:13.

8. God promises to make me a good student. His Word tells me that school will never get so hard that I can't get a passing grade. God tells me that He will help me Himself if I obey and listen to Him. I know that God has given me my parents—and even my teacher—to help me pass a class in which I have a hard time.

# SOCIAL STUDIES
## Grade 5

### BIBLICAL CONCEPT
Godly love is not influenced by an individual's response, but by the Word of God and the Holy Spirit's leading, as it relates to our relationship with Him.

### PSYCHOLOGICAL CONCEPT
An individual's behavior toward another is influenced by how that other individual behaves toward him/her.

### BIBLICALLY INTEGRATED CONCEPT
An individual's godly behavior is motivated by the Word of God, the Holy Spirit and his/her relationship of God's love, his/her experience of God's love rather than the behavior of others.

### BACKGROUND INFORMATION FOR TEACHING BIC
Jesus, in Matthew 5:43-48 says that we should be like God, who is perfect, loving those who hate us. In Galatians 5:16, Paul tells us to "walk in the Spirit and ye shall not fulfill the lust of the flesh." When we are walking with the Lord, we will not react to others in a fleshly way. In Ephesians, Paul tells us to be kind to each other, forgiving each other because God has forgiven us. He goes on to say that we are to walk in love, as Christ has loved us.

### LEADING TO LIFE INTEGRATION
Motivations for Relating to Others:
    A. Love
    B. Duty
    C. Authority
    D. Vocational

# SOCIAL STUDIES
## Grade 6

### BIBLICAL CONCEPT
God's design is for all men to be rightly related to Him and be responsive to His control of one's behavior.

### PSYCHOLOGICAL CONCEPT
An individual has control over and is responsible for his/her own behavior.

## BIBLICALLY INTEGRATED CONCEPT

God through His Word and the ministry of the Holy Spirit has provided the means for an individual to control his behavior, though each person is individually responsible before God.

## BACKGROUND INFORMATION FOR TEACHING THE BIC

Colossians 3:5—Mortify your members.
Colossians 3:17—Do in word or deed, do to the glory of God.
1 Corinthians 9:27—Bring your body under subjection.
Philippians 2:5—Mind of Jesus.
Philippians 4:6, 7, 19—Supply your needs, hearts and minds in Christ Jesus.
John 14:24—Peace I give to you.
Galatians 5:22—Love, joy, peace, longsuffering, etc.

## LEADING TO LIFE INTEGRATION

Emphasis should be placed upon developing personal responsibility within the:

A. Family
B. Community
C. State
D. Nation
E. World
F. Church

# SOCIAL STUDIES

## Kindergarten

### BIBLICAL CONCEPT

God is sovereign even though because of the Fall not all events, traditions, and customs immediately honor God.

### HISTORICAL CONCEPT

Events, traditions, and customs have roots in the past.

### BIBLICALLY INTEGRATED CONCEPT

God is in control of events, traditions and customs, past, present and future and all history will ultimately honor God
(Daniel 2:21).

**BACKGROUND INFORMATION FOR TEACHING THE BIC**
Genesis chapters 37-45—The jealousy Joseph's brothers had for him was not pleasing to God. But God used it to save their lives (Genesis 45:5).

Ephesians 1:11—All history is within God's control and He is working out "everything in conformity with the purpose of His will."

# SOCIAL STUDIES
## Grade 1

### BIBLICAL CONCEPT
God is immutable and thus a stabilizer in the middle of change.

### HISTORICAL CONCEPT
Change is always occurring.

### BIBLICALLY INTEGRATED CONCEPT
In the face of a changing world, it is reassuring to know that God is aware of our changes, though He never changes. He is a stabilizing force.

**BACKGROUND INFORMATION FOR TEACHING THE BIC**
The Bible teaches in James 1:17, and many other portions of Scripture teach that God does not change. If you are going to use the term immutable with the first graders it must be simply defined with some good illustrations that the children can grasp. Also the idea that everything else changes needs to be adequately explained so that the child can know that God is totally different from anything and everyone else in the fact that He is completely unchangable.

**LEADING TO LIFE INTEGRATION**
God works all things after the counsel of His own will. God will help us grow up to please Him.

# SOCIAL STUDIES
## Grade 2

### BIBLICAL CONCEPT
Life as God created it involves growth.

### HISTORICAL CONCEPT
Because change is always occurring, life in any community differs from its past.

## BIBLICALLY INTEGRATED CONCEPT

The work of God in a community will usually cause beneficial growth, thus communities are constantly changing.

## BACKGROUND INFORMATION FOR TEACHING THE BIC

As the physical body needs food to grow, so does our spiritual being. Humans are created in God's image. God desires to see growth in His children.

## LEADING TO LIFE INTEGRATION

The Word of God in a community will cause beneficial growth. In Deuteronomy it talks about desiring the sincere milk of the Word that we would grow thereby. In the social strata, God's work (with the Word) changes and causes growth—both in numerical converts and spiritual benefits for humanity.

# SOCIAL STUDIES
## Grade 3

### BIBLICAL CONCEPT
God has created man with ability to think rationally.

### HISTORICAL CONCEPT
Change in any community is often the result of technological advancement and this change is often evident in methods of transportation, communication, and urbanization.

## BIBLICALLY INTEGRATED CONCEPT

Because God has provided man with the ability to think rationally, technological advancement is evident in methods of transportation, communication and urbanization.

## BACKGROUND INFORMATION FOR TEACHING THE BIC

The God who created the universe, has given man dominion over the creation. This gives man a unique ability to use the creation. This ability demonstrates man's creation by God. It has allowed him to advance far beyond any of the other creatures. This advancement is very evident in technology.

## LEADING TO LIFE INTEGRATION

God who created the universe, has created man in His own image with many abilities including thought and reason. Due to this God-given ability man is able to subdue the creation, which God has given man to rule. Thus due to

God's plan, man is over creatures and able to make new and better advancements in every field.

# SOCIAL STUDIES
## Grade 4

### BIBLICAL CONCEPT
God deals with man on the basis of past events.

### HISTORICAL CONCEPT
The historical past influences the present and the present cannot be adequately understood without knowledge of the past.

### BIBLICALLY INTEGRATED CONCEPT
To know the present, we must know how God has dealt with man in the past.

### BACKGROUND INFORMATION FOR TEACHING THE BIC
Understanding of man's present condition demands our research in the area of redemptive history as seen in the Scriptures. Man's creation and fall have affected us all throughout human history. Man's struggle is always centered around finding fulfillment and purpose in life. His purpose is found in God's truth (Word), and its relationship to man's past.

### LEADING TO LIFE INTEGRATION
My sin is a result of Adam's.
The wars of history are a result of the fall.
God cared for Israel, He cares for me and will guide my path if I let him.

# SOCIAL STUDIES
## Grade 5

### BIBLICAL CONCEPT
Sin has caused conflict.

### HISTORICAL CONCEPT
Because change is always occurring, confict may result, but differences can be resolved in different ways.

### BIBLICALLY INTEGRATED CONCEPT
God has provided principles by which man can cope with change and resolve personal conflicts.

## BACKGROUND INFORMATION FOR TEACHING THE BIC

God, in His love, has provided the necessary requirement for sin's results. John 3:16—The sacrifice of His Son saves all who put their trust in Him. God has given us His Word to be used by His Spirit to teach us as we search out the principles for living. These principles are the true foundation that results in success in life.

Romans 8:28—God works in the lives of people, placing them into situations where they can learn and grow. Example: Paul and Silas were thrown in prison and their response was one of praise resulting in salvation of the jailer and his household (Acts 16). Negative example: Cain and Abel's conflict over a sacrifice resulting in Abel being murdered. Cain was not in fellowship and practicing the principles God set down.

Genesis 37—Joseph's conflict with his brothers resulted in his being transported to Egypt as a slave. God worked in this situation to exalt Joseph as he sought the Lord and lived according to His will.

# SOCIAL STUDIES

## Grade 6

### BIBLICAL CONCEPT

God has given man a conscience.

### HISTORICAL CONCEPT

History demonstrates that people have been motivated by values and ideals and by material wants and needs.

### BIBLICALLY INTEGRATED CONCEPT

Man's God-given conscience motivates him to support certain ideals and values.

## BACKGROUND INFORMATION FOR TEACHING THE BIC

The Bible teaches that, since man is God's creation in His own image, he has certain intrinsic values. The belief in a divine being who rewards and punishes has given man a foundation by which to judge. The conscience then is molded by this belief. The belief may be true or false. The conscience, therefore, can be taught truth or error. The ideals and values may be proper or not.

# SOCIAL STUDIES
## Kindergarten

**BIBLICAL CONCEPT**

God has given man the responsibility for caring for the creation.

**ECONOMIC CONCEPT**

A person cannot totally satisfy material wants, because the wants of humans are unlimited, whereas the resources needed to fulfill these wants are limited.

**BIBLICALLY INTEGRATED CONCEPT**

In God's world man has all the available resources he needs to live an abundant life.

### BACKGROUND INFORMATION FOR TEACHING THE BIC

Matthew 6: 25-34

God takes care of plants and animals.

Man is more important to God than plants and animals.

Worrying and anxiety cannot help our needs.

Man must seek God first.

### LEADING TO LIFE INTEGRATION

Emphasis should be placed on the following available resources:

Money

Trade

Self-sufficiency

In a basic way teach the children their responsibility to care for God's creation (such as animal life and plant life).

Also demonstrate through visuals the pollution problems and other abuses which man has brought upon his environment.

# SOCIAL STUDIES
## Grade 1

**BIBLICAL CONCEPT**

God knows what man needs even before man makes his requests known, and promises to meet those needs.

**ECONOMIC CONCEPT**

As a consumer, an individual must decide which needs will be met and which will not be satisfied.

## BIBLICALLY INTEGRATED CONCEPT

God knows our needs and can cause us to be content that He will meet those needs.

## BACKGROUND INFORMATION FOR TEACHING THE BIC

God has promised that if we will present ourselves to Him (Romans 12:1, 2; Proverbs 3:5, 6), He will guide us. He already knows our needs, even before we ask (Matthew 6:8). He has promised to meet those needs (Philippians 4:19). Therefore, we can rest contented in the fact that God will meet those needs (Philippians 4:12; Matthew 6:25-34 especially v. 33).

## LEADING TO LIFE INTEGRATION

God exhorts us to be good stewards and not waste what He has given to us. We need to carefully budget ourselves and pray for God's will in all things. We should not grieve over what we do not have, but be content with what God has given us (Hebrews 13:5).

The needs of the Christian are different from the unsaved. The Christian's eyes are focused and dependent on God and the eyes of the unsaved are focused on the world. God exhorts us to be good stewards of our things. He also teaches through Paul's writings, that we should learn, whatever state we are in, to be content. Therefore, if we are not able to get certain things, they may not be necessarily needs, but rather wants.

God exhorts us to be good stewards—responsible, sensible, faithful (Luke 16:1-13). God tells us that we should be content with what we have (Hebrews 13:5), for he will never leave us or forsake us (Hebrews 13:5). He promises that if we seek first His kingdom, that all these things (needs) shall be given to us (Matthew 6:24-34).

Johnny wanted very badly to go to the social outing with the group from school. He did not have the money and his parents could not help. Johnny was able to work with a retired man across the street. This provided more than enough money to pay for the outing. Johnny's Mom and Dad helped Johnny see how God met his need.

# SOCIAL STUDIES
## Grade 2

### BIBLICAL CONCEPT

God has endowed each individual with certain aptitudes, interests, and capacities according to the good pleasure of His will through which he can accomplish God's will.

### ECONOMIC CONCEPT

In a work-oriented society individuals perform specialized tasks to provide goods and services for themselves and others.

## BIBLICALLY INTEGRATED CONCEPT

God's design for successful living involves the individual's accurate perception of his God-given aptitudes and capacities given so that he might glorify God and perform specialized tasks needed by society.

## BACKGROUND INFORMATION FOR TEACHING THE BIC

Romans 12
Ephesians 4
1 Corinthians 12-14
Parable of the Talents
Also the fact that we are created in God's image

## LEADING TO LIFE INTEGRATION

Physical
Energy
Transportation
Education
Welfare

# SOCIAL STUDIES
## Grade 3

### BIBLICAL CONCEPT

God measures success in terms of what an individual has done with his God-given aptitudes and capacities as to what he could have done with them.

### ECONOMIC CONCEPT

Specialization increases productivity and leads to increased interdependence among individuals and communities.

## BIBLICALLY INTEGRATED CONCEPT

Utilizing one's God-given aptitudes and capacities to their fullest potential increases an individual's productivity and expands his sphere of ministry to others.

## BACKGROUND INFORMATION FOR TEACHING THE BIC

The concept of lost reward—1 Corinthians 3:13-16—We will be judged based on what we could have done.

The concept of gifts given to individuals for ministry to others in the body—
Romans 12; 1 Corinthians 12; and Ephesians 4.
We have nothing and are nothing save what God has given us.

## LEADING TO LIFE INTEGRATION
Emphasis should be placed on:
Increasing resources
Recognizing skills and aptitudes
Developing skills and aptitudes
Financial planning involved in buying goods and services.

# SOCIAL STUDIES
## Grade 4

### BIBLICAL CONCEPT
God provides financial freedom for those who observe the principles of His Word.

### ECONOMIC CONCEPT
The patterns of buying and selling in a country or region depend on available resources and the educational and technological development of its people.

### BIBLICALLY INTEGRATED CONCEPT
Decisions regarding how one uses the resources God has given him are to be made on the basis of wisdom and understanding gleaned from obedience to God's Word.

## BACKGROUND INFORMATION FOR TEACHING THE BIC
Biblical Exhortations and Warnings Regarding Money:
For the love of money is the root of all evil: which while some coveted after, they have erred from the faith, and pierced themselves through with many sorrows (1 Timothy 6:10).
The rich are not to be highminded. The rich are to do good and be rich in good works (1 Timothy 6:17, 18).
Covetousness is placed among the gross sins (1 Corinthians 6:9-10 and Colossians 3:5).
General warning to the rich (James 5:1-6).
Lay up treasures of a spiritual nature (Matthew 6:19-21).
Are to seek first the kingdom of God . . . and these things (cf. context) shall be added (Matthew 6:33).

Seek those things above. Set your affections on things above (Colossians 3:1, 2).

The parable of the Rich Fool (Luke 12:13-21).

The parable of the Unjust Steward (Luke 16:1-13).

The parable of Rich Young Ruler (Luke 18:18-24).

The parable of the Ten Pounds (Luke 19-11-24).

Provision is to be made for the family (1 Timothy 5:8).

## LEADING TO LIFE INTEGRATION

Relation of Financial Adeptness to Eligibility for Church Office:

1. A bishop is not to be a lover of money (1 Timothy 3:3; Titus 1:7).
2. A deacon is not to be greedy of filthy lucre (1 Timothy 3:8).
3. A bishop must be blameless as God's steward (Titus 1:7).
4. A bishop must rule his own house well (i.e. finances) (1 Timothy 3:4).

# SOCIAL STUDIES

## Grade 5

### BIBLICAL CONCEPT

God provides financial freedom for those who observe the principles of His Word.

### ECONOMIC CONCEPT

The patterns of buying and selling in a country or region depend on available resources and the educational and technological development of its people.

### BIBLICALLY INTEGRATED CONCEPT

Decisions regarding how one uses the resources God has given him are to be made on the basis of wisdom and understanding gleaned from obedience to God's Word.

## LEADING TO LIFE INTEGRATION

Because God is in control of the patterns of buying and selling, we have no need to worry about our provision (Philippians 4:13).

God has sovereignly bestowed a different measure of available resources, educational and technological development upon each country or region.

God is ultimately responsible for all patterns of buying and selling, because he has sovereignly bestowed the availability of all resources.

# SOCIAL STUDIES
## Grade 6

### BIBLICAL CONCEPT

God desires that all men first seek after godliness rather than the accumulation of wealth and possessions.

### ECONOMIC CONCEPT

Economic systems are shaped by the values and traditions of the culture.

### BIBLICALLY INTEGRATED CONCEPT

God desires that each individual within a culture make economic decisions consistent with the principles of His Word, so that the economic system itself gives evidence of values and traditions compatible with a Christian world view.

### LEADING TO LIFE INTEGRATION

Do a comparison or contrast of today's view of what success is in relationship to the biblical concept.

1. It would be appropriate to look at current economic trends and philosophies and compare them with the Word of God. This would be done to show where the principles are not biblically based.
2. Do a study of cultures where the government failed because of corruption, and show how the economic system suffered.
3. Show how following principles of God's Word can help a culture economically.
4. Today's inflation is a result of greed among individuals in our society.
5. There is dishonesty and a lack of conviction in our society concerning economic policy and the handling of the nations income to benefit only a select segment of our society.

# SOCIAL STUDIES
## Kindergarten

### BIBLICAL CONCEPT

God commanded men to love one another.

### POLITICAL SCIENCE CONCEPT

Rules are necessary to protect the individual.

## BIBLICALLY INTEGRATED CONCEPT

God desires that men should treat one another as they themselves wish to be treated (Matthew 7— The Golden Rule).

## LEADING TO LIFE INTEGRATION

The students will help set their standards for the treatment of each other in the classroom (with teacher supervision) to be in harmony with Matthew 7.

The family should set household standards in harmony with Matthew 7.

The family should teach these principles to other families as they live a life pleasing to God.

Emphasis should be placed on:
1. Rules for classroom behavior
2. Rules in the family
3. Rules in the city or town

# SOCIAL STUDIES
## Grade 1

### BIBLICAL CONCEPT

God has ordained the family unit as the vehicle for the instruction and discipline of the young.

### POLITICAL SCIENCE CONCEPT

Rules are necessary to govern the behavior of individuals within groups.

### BIBLICALLY INTEGRATED CONCEPT

God's design for the family includes the instruction and discipline of children through both verbal instruction and modeling consistent with God's righteous character.

## BACKGROUND INFORMATION FOR TEACHING THE BIC

Deuteronomy 6:6-7
Ephesians 6:3
Psalm 119:7-8—Righteous judgments based on God's Word.

## LEADING TO LIFE INTEGRATION

Emphasis should be placed on:
1. The definition of a rule
2. Where rules come from
3. Why rules are necessary

# SOCIAL STUDIES
## Grade 2

### BIBLICAL CONCEPT

God's Word sets forth the precepts which children are to be taught and delegates to the parents the responsibility for instruction and reproof.

### POLITICAL SCIENCE CONCEPT

The members of a family are governed by a system of rules which specify positions of authority and procedures for enforcing rules.

### BIBLICALLY INTEGRATED CONCEPT

God's design for the family involves precise instruction in godly conduct and obedience to those family members in authority.

### BACKGROUND INFORMATION FOR TEACHING THE BIC

Need for authority—God knows and chooses a leader who will rule over us (Ephesians 5:23).

Need for obedience. The Bible says children must be obedient to the authority of parents.

Community laws must be put to action and should not be broken because it is still part of God's order of life to keep the law. Example: Ten Commandments and Exodus 20.

### LEADING TO LIFE INTEGRATION

Emphasis should be placed upon:
1. Need for authority
2. Need for obedience
3. Community laws

# SOCIAL STUDIES
## Grade 3

### BIBLICAL CONCEPT

Government is ordained by God who has endowed certain individuals with a capacity for leadership.

### POLITICAL SCIENCE CONCEPT

The purpose of government is to protect and serve the needs of its citizens.

## BIBLICALLY INTEGRATED CONCEPT

God allows certain individuals to assume positions of leadership and authority in order that His purposes for the community might be accomplished.

## BACKGROUND INFORMATION FOR TEACHING THE BIC

Jesus Christ recognized the difference between political and spiritual responsibilities. In an attempt to trap our Lord, the Pharisees asked, "Is it acceptable to pay tribute or taxes to the government?" God's Word is clear that governments are ordained of God. Rulers are placed in positions of responsibility ultimately by God. Christians are not above the law, for to resist authority is to oppose the ordinance of God. Rules are a minister of God for good not evil. Christians are to be submissive to the governing authorities (Matthew 22:15-22; Mark 12:13-17; Luke 20:20-26; Romans 13:1-14 [esp. 1-4]; 1 Peter 2:13-17 [esp. 13, 14]).

## LEADING TO LIFE INTEGRATION

Emphasis should be placed on:
1. Types of authorities
2. Kinds of governments with different types of authorities
3. Ways leaders are selected
4. Leadership qualities

# SOCIAL STUDIES
## Grade 4

### BIBLICAL CONCEPT

God desires that men live peaceably with one another in an attitude of love after the manner of Christ.

### POLITICAL SCIENCE CONCEPT

Peaceful interaction within and between communities depends on a formal system of social control.

### BIBLICALLY INTEGRATED CONCEPT

Christ-like character facilitates a system of social control that stems from personal submission to God rather than formal controls of any social system.

## BACKGROUND INFORMATION FOR TEACHING THE BIC
Strife comes because men have inner conflict (James 4:1, 2).

Unity comes from maintaining the mind of Christ (Philippians 2:1-16).

Love for God and love for our brothers go hand in hand and are inseparable (1 John 4:16-21).

The ability to love and forgive others is made possible by God's love and forgiveness for us (Ephesians 4:20-32).

Unity of relationships and submission to one another come from submission to God (Colossians 3:1).

# SOCIAL STUDIES

## Grade 5

### BIBLICAL CONCEPT
God has created man with the freedom to choose and it is His desire that men choose to live together in peace and in ultimate submission to His will.

### POLITICAL SCIENCE CONCEPT
The pattern of government for a group of communities is determined by the degree to which the governed participate in the political system.

### BIBLICALLY INTEGRATED CONCEPT
In His sovereignty God has allowed men to establish governments and He seeks to accomplish His purpose through the political systems they set up.

### LEADING TO LIFE INTEGRATION
Emphasis should be placed upon participation of the governed in these differing systems of government.

Tribal
Kingdom
Empire
Feudalism
Dictatorships
Democracy
Theocracy

# SOCIAL STUDIES
## Grade 6

### BIBLICAL CONCEPT

Consistent godly living makes it possible for all men to live together in accordance with God's purpose.

### POLITICAL SCIENCE CONCEPT

Stable political organization improves the quality of life shared by its citizens.

### BIBLICALLY INTEGRATED CONCEPT

God's blessing on a political unit (a nation) is determined by the degree to which its political system is based upon and adheres to the principles of God's Word.

### BACKGROUND INFORMATION FOR TEACHING THE BIC

The whole section of Paul's letter to the Romans in chapter 13 talks about the need for every man to submit to the governing authorities. The reason given is that there is no authority which God has not instituted. God says that when we rebel against the authorities we are actually rebelling against God. Further, Paul says these authorities are there for our good to help those who do right. God says to pay taxes due the government.

### LEADING TO LIFE INTEGRATION

We find personal blessings if we walk in obedience to God by walking in submission to the government over us. When Israel walked according to God's principles, God blessed the people. But when as a nation Israel turned away from these principles, He sent judgment. "Blessed is the nation whose God is the Lord."

# SUGGESTED SPECIFIC CONTENT FOR TEACHING LIFE STUDIES

This suggested specific content is the contribution of Christian school teachers K-6 in the following schools:

1. Norfolk Christian School, Norfolk, Virginia
2. Delaware County Christian School, Newtown Square, Pennsylvania
3. Scottsdale Christian Academy, Scottsdale, Arizona
4. The Christian Academy, Bookview, Pennsylvania
5. First Baptist Academy, Dallas, Texas

# KINDERGARTEN

## CONCEPTS TO BE TAUGHT:

Five senses
Creation - nature
Seasons
Family
Feelings - others' and own
Self acceptance
Responsibility
Climate
Weather
Calendar
Other school personnel
Health concepts
Developing understanding of self and others:
  Understanding and accepting self
  Understanding feelings
  Understanding others
  Understanding independence
  Understanding goals and purposeful behavior
  Understanding mastery, competence, resourcefulness
  Understanding emotional maturity
  Understanding choices and consequences
Flag (Christian and American)
Missions
Holidays - Columbus Day, Halloween, Thanksgiving, Christmas, Valentine's Day, Lincoln's Birthday, Washington's Birthday, St. Patrick's Day, Easter (Not all of these are acceptable to all Christians).
The School Community - people involved in our buildings: teachers, clerks, nurse, librarians. Also trips to each to see projects, plays, programs. Visits to our class by some of the people (band director, etc.).

# FIRST GRADE

## CONTENT AND/OR CONCEPTS TO BE TAUGHT:

Science, health, and social studies are integrated in first grade. We do not have a text; we do use "Weekly Reader."

## MAJOR OBJECTIVES:

1. To teach children that God has placed them in school, as He had previously placed them in a family.

2. To teach pupils the interdependence of home, school, and themselves.

3. To teach students to see the works of God in the physical features of their environment.

4. To teach facts from observation about plants, animals, seasons, etc.

5. To teach the children the importance of cleanliness and nutrition.

We also study famous people and events which have happened; and present happenings of importance.

## I. Goals
A. Develop understanding of families living within a community.
B. Understand that people live in different types of dwellings, but have the same needs.
C. See that people living together serve one another.
D. Recognize the family's dependence on community helpers.
E. Examine the services offered within one's own community.

## II. Content
A. Units
1. The ways people live (housing, customs)
2. Needs of all families (shelter, spiritual, health, food, etc.)
3. A community - what is it?
4. Community helpers and services:
   a. The farm
   b. Police and safety
   c. Library
   d. Transportation - land, sea, air
   e. The church
B. Supplementary Units
1. Map of classroom and school
2. Missions
3. Famous Americans

## III. Methods
A. Group discussion
B. Field trips
C. Games
D. Observations

# SECOND GRADE

The second grade is a "social" study in itself and is treated as such. Manners, fairness, coping with victory and defeat, sharing toys, etc., expressing thoughts and ideas, voting (could be part of fairness), and just plain living together are all taught throughout the year.

The Bible times lend themselves very nicely to social studies and we use those times to compare with ours. For example, much of the land was the same as that in Arizona.

Any states or foreign lands visited by the teachers provide excellent pictures and facts to be shared with the students. The students always seem to enjoy hearing about things the teachers have seen and done.

## CONTENT AND/OR CONCEPTS TO BE TAUGHT:
Community life
   Community workers
   Communities of long ago
   Farms - Towns, cities
   Community services
   Transportation and communication
   Community Government
Maps and their symbols
Using a globe
The earth and the sun
Warm land communities - Hawaii, Mexico, Puerto Rico
Cold land communities - Alaska, Norway
Cities around the world - Amsterdam, Tokyo, London
America
   The flag
   Citizenship
   Special places in America

## I. Goals
   A.  Broaden understanding of the services a community offers
   B.  Discover the interdependency of people within a community and between communities
   C.  Understand the concept of a city and its make-up
   D.  Develop an understanding of how God uses us to spread the news of the Gospel within the community
   E.  Understand basic map concepts
   F.  Study map of home state and city
   G.  Realize that a city is part of a state (concept of state)
   H.  Examine the activities and services of a state

## II. Content
   A.  Units
       1.  Community services:
          a.  Parks
          b.  Medical
          c.  Communications (postal, newspaper, T.V., phone, etc.)

      2. Special services
        a. Military
        b. Educational - schools and colleges, museums
        c. Job opportunities - ship building, bakery, banks, etc.
      3. Map study - basic skills - city, state
      4. Study concept of state
      5. State Services
  B. Supplementary Units
      1. Missions
      2. Famous Americans

**III. Methods**
  A. Discussion
  B. Projects
  C. Field Trips
  D. Films

# THIRD GRADE

## CONTENT AND/OR CONCEPTS TO BE TAUGHT:
Map skills
The Sinai Peninsula
Palestine (time of Christ)
Greece (time of Paul's missionary journeys)
Economics: How are goods and services produced?
           How do people in metropolitan areas get the things they want?
Human Geography: Where do men build cities?
              How do people use natural resources?
              How do metropolitan areas grow?
Physical Geography: Why are metropolitan areas located where they are?
Modern Israel

## I. Goals
  A. To gain an understanding of various periods in American history.
  B. To become more aware of the geography of America.
  C. To understand that history is really "His Story," and to recognize God's work in the development of America.
  D. To appreciate the high values in American culture, including individual freedom, truth, justice, respect for property of others, and loyalty to God, country, family, and self.
  E. To develop an appreciation and love for our country.
  F. To further develop map and globe skills.

**II. Content**
   A. Colonial America
      1. Anglo-America before the Europeans came
      2. Explorers come to the new world
      3. Making new homes in Anglo-America
      4. Living in Colonial America
   B. The Colonies become a nation
      1. The French and Indian War
      2. The War for Independence
      3. The New Nation
   C. The Nation Expands
      1. Settling mid-America
      2. Settling the far West
      3. The Great Plains
      4. The far North
   D. Industry and Cities in Anglo-America
      1. The end of slavery
      2. Industry grows in Anglo-America
      3. Cities grow in Anglo-America
**III. Methods**
   A. Discussion
   B. Films
   C. Field Trips
   D. Research and reports

**SAMPLE CURRICULUM:**
I. Communities
   A. People in communities
   B. Communities Change
   C. Communities around the World
   D. Understanding each other - how communities are alike and different
II. "Colonial Life" in America
   A. Pilgrims - Mayflower, Plymouth
   B. Patriots - Revolutionary War, Concord, Lexington, Boston, Philadel-
      phia, Paul Revere, Washington, Patrick Henry, Jefferson, Franklin,
      Betsy Ross.
   C. Early Pioneers - where they moved from, where they moved to, their
      way of life.
III. Indians - their customs, homes, food, relationship with "white" men
   A. Of the Southwest - Navaho and Pueblo
   B. Of the Woodlands
   C. Of the Northwest
   D. Of the Plains

IV. Geography of the United States
   A. The Oceans
   B. The Rivers
   C. Geographical areas: East, West, North, South
   D. Mountain Ranges
   E. Dialects within our Country (and Class)
   F. Customs
   G. Climates
   H. Time differences
V. State History and Geography (An overview)
   A. Early origin of our state - original inhabitants
   B. Explorers to influence our state
   C. Statehood
   D. State symbol, flag, flower, bird
   E. State officials presently holding office
   F. Geography - desert, mountains, rivers, special points of interest
   G. Our contribution as a state to the nation - characteristics of our state

# FOURTH GRADE

## CONTENT AND/OR CONCEPTS TO BE TAUGHT:
The following is based on a Scott, Foresman text, *Investigating Man's World: Regional Studies*, 1970. This is a conceptually structured program organized according to the key concepts and generalizations of anthropology, economics, history, political science, geography and sociology.

Explorers - French, English, Dutch, Spanish
Colonies - New England, Middle, Southern, The Frontier
Revolutionary War
Settling the West
Inventors

## I. Goals
   A. To give an understanding of how God has worked in the past and is working His will out in history today.
   B. To show the relationship of people with each other and with their environment and the reasons why people live as they do.
   C. To bring about a better understanding of the interrelationships of sociology, economics, political science in our state, country and world.
   D. To study the way of life of a people as they worked together to solve their problems.
   E. To develop further the skills in using maps, pictures, globes and graphs.
   F. To learn of past struggles, asperations, success and failures of people of various cultures and how they influence us today.

**II. Content**
  A. Investigating Man's World
   1. Physical Geography
   2. Anthropology - early man
   3. Sociology
   4. Economics
   5. Political science - state and national emphasis
   6. Human Geography
   7. History - state and national emphasis
   8. Overview - Switzerland, Ghana, Great Lakes, Midwest, Virginia
**III. Methods**
  A. Discussion
  B. Projects
  C. Interviews
  D. Resource people
  E. Pictures
**IV. Study of a state**
  A. Physical Geography
   1. Spatial location (map skills: land and water areas: hemisphere, continent, country, state; oceans, seas, rivers, lakes; latitude and longitude; map symbols and scale of miles
   2. Territory
   3. Natural Setting
   4. Natural Resources
  B. Anthropology
   1. Way of Life
   2. Early Man
   3. Races of Man
   4. Culture and Cultural Change
  C. Sociology
   1. Population
   2. Groups of People
   3. Change
  D. Economics
   1. Money
   2. Market System
   3. Public Expenditure and Income
   4. Budget
  E. Political Science
   1. Constitutional Government
   2. Authority
   3. Citizenship
   4. Laws
   5. Politics

F. Human Geography
   1. Population Density
   2. Commercial Agriculture
   3. Manufacturing and Transportation
G. History
   1. Events
   2. Natural, Political, Economic and Social Factors

# FIFTH GRADE

## CONTENT AND/OR CONCEPTS TO BE TAUGHT:
Map Skills
Exploration of America
Colonization of America
American Revolution
Westward Movement
Industry, economics, anthropology of states today
The fifty states
The Civil War
Presidents
Canada
Mexico

# SIXTH GRADE

Old World history with an introduction to general geography skills and map reading, graphs, etc.

## Concepts:
   1. Physical Geography
      a. Spatial location
      b. Natural setting
      c. Natural resources
   2. History
      a. Natural factors
      b. Political factors
      c. Economic factors
      d. Social factors
   3. Anthropology
      a. Early Man
      b. Races of Man
      c. Culture

4. Sociology
    a. Population
    b. Society
    c. Social Change
5. Economics
    a. Economic system
    b. Money, credit, banking
    c. Role of government
    d. Economic growth
6. Political Science
    a. Constitutional government
    b. Citizenship
    c. Laws
    d. Politics
7. Human Geography
    a. Population distribution
    b. Commercial agriculture
    c. Commercial forestry
    d. Commercial fishing
    e. Manufacturing
    f. Transportation system

**Map Skills**
1. Review of directions
2. Landforms
3. Waterforms
4. Latitude
5. Longitude
6. Mileage scale, legends
7. The earth's surface
8. The earth's climates
9. Political maps
10. Other maps

**Content**
1. Western hemisphere
2. Latin America
3. Latitude and longitude
4. North and South America compared
5. Landforms of Latin America
6. Climate regions of Latin America
7. Altitude and climate of Latin America
8. Countries of Latin America
9. Waterways of Latin America
10. Major cities and Population of Latin America
11. Capitals of Latin America

12. Rainfall of Latin America
13. Vegetation of Latin America
14. Farming and grazing of Latin America
15. Minerals of Latin America
16. Mexico

## Latin America

1. Central America
2. Panama Canal
3. Venezuela
4. Colombia
5. Brazil
6. Paraguay
7. Argentina
8. Uruguay
9. Chile
10. Peru
11. Ecuador
12. Bolivia

## Review

## SAMPLE CURRICULUM:

I. Genesis
    A. Beginning of World - Creation, etc.
        1. General study in character of God
        2. Fall of man - consequences
    B. Noah and flood
    C. Mesopotamian Civilization: Tower of Babel, Babylon, Assyria, Phoenicia, Bible Books of Daniel, Ezra, Nehemiah, etc. (very general).
        1. Abraham
        2. Isaac
        3. Jacob
        4. Joseph
II. The Pentateuch
    A. Ancient Egypt
        1. Moses
        2. The Wanderings of Israel
III. Joshua & the Judges
    A. Joshua (Battle of Jericho, etc.)
    B. Judges
        1. Deborah
        2. Gideon
        3. Samson
        4. Samuel

IV. Kingdom of Nation Israel
   A. Saul
   B. David
   C. Solomon - Division of Nation
V. Ancient Greece
VI. Ancient Rome
   A. Birth of Christ and Christianity
   B. Early Missionaries, etc.
VII. Middle Ages

1. Dr. Daniel Noonan, *Drug Interactions With Alcohol* cassette series 400-6, 1972.
2. Ibid.
3. Price, *Jesus the Teacher*, p.2.

# CHAPTER 9

# Life Integration: The Application Step in Teaching-Learning

Often when discussing the subject of practical application of Scripture with teachers, one is confronted with such statements as "My responsibility is to just teach the Word; it's the Holy Spirit's job to apply it." The pious nature of such a statement almost makes any disagreement sound sacriligious. "God only tells us to give out His Word. His Spirit will do the rest. He promises that His Word will not return to Him void." Supported by such wonderful biblical phraseology, it almost seems that the discussion has ended. But is such a philosophy consistent with the Bible? If the Holy Spirit uses the human element as His instrument to *present* truth, might He not also wish to use the same instrument to *apply* the truth. If you have made your students memorize biblical facts, has your responsibility ended?

The thrust of this chapter is to examine both the biblical and educational foundations for relating biblical truth to life, and then examine the area of methodology and evaluate several in light of their potential to be used to relate Scripture to students' lives. Finally, some principles for life application will be suggested.

## Biblical Foundation

The teacher who just "teaches the Word," concerned primarily with the content and cognitive learning should take a good long look at the nature of the Book they are teaching. Are we teaching our students to take God at his Word, to "hide God's Word in our hearts (lives)" or just to take the words as God's and hide them in our head (mind).

Richards reminds us that:

> In the Bible God presents truth, true information, from and about Himself. But God does more, He presents Himself in the information. God Himself confronts us in His truth. When a person meets God, a response is always called for . . . This is one of the basic problems of the Evangelical. We see the Word of God as revealed, as true information from God. And so it is. But we tend to see it as information only! We neglect the personal dimension. . . . No reader of the Bible can escape it. Response *is* essential. It is never enough just to have information about God.[1]

God could have written an inspired, systematic theology textbook, but he did not. He could have dictated all of Scripture directly and not bothered with human authors, but He did not choose to do so. The Bible has come to us by and through real men in real life, because God never intended that doctrinal truth should ever be divorced from life. To approach a Bible teaching situation or for that matter any teaching in a Christian context from a factual viewpoint only, to be concerned only with observation and interpretation or the cataloging of facts, information, and never with application, is, in the words of Professor Hendricks a "spiritual abortion."

A thoughtful look at the Holy Spirit's ministry will also show the fallacy of the "I-just-teach-the-Word" syndrome. The writer of Hebrews (4:12) states, "For the Word of God is alive" or really "Living is the Word of God." Even though the Word is alive it does not always produce life, and certainly the dynamic of the Holy Spirit's ministry is crucial but not the only determining factor. The fact that it is the Holy Spirit's ministry to relate truth to life does not mean that the human teacher can ignore life application. The Holy Spirit is not a maid, going about tidying up after sloppy teachers. In 1 Corinthians 3:6, Paul speaks of both the divine and human elements: "I planted, Apollos watered, but God was causing the growth." The teacher who "just teaches the Word" and expects the Holy Spirit to do all the rest could be compared to a farmer who says, "Since God is the only one who can make a seed grow, I don't need to prepare the soil, properly plant, fertilize and if necessary irrigate, I'll just dump the seeds on the ground and let Him do the rest." Zuck expresses it thus:

> It is erroneous for teachers to suppose that all they need to do is unfold Scripture and let the Holy Spirit apply it where it is needed. There is a dangerous half-truth in such a statement. True, the Holy Spirit does apply to the experience the truth that has been taught. But He does so only with truth that has been chosen discriminately with relation to life-needs and in cases where the heart soil has been prepared to receive the seed of the Word of God. Scriptural truths scattered indiscriminately will inevitably fall on stony ground, thorny ground, or "by the wayside." Bible truths chosen and presented by teachers on the basis of life-needs and on prepared "soil" can be used to the fullest by the Spirit.[2]

The problem we are dealing with is not the *place* or authority of the Bible in Christian education, but the *use* of the Bible in Christian education and specifically in our own lives. It is true that there has been a tremendous battle for the Bible in relationship to the inspiration and authority (inerrancy) of the Scriptures. It used to be said that our position was verbal plenary inspiration but then some felt that the word plenary was unnecessary. If one believed in verbal inspiration some could choose to apply that to all of the Scriptures where others could take a more limited perspective and that way it would help to unify us in the body of Christ rather than divide us. However, the word plenary relates to the fact that the Bible is authoritative and inerrant in its entirety. The word plenary is absolutely essential. Later the position was taken that the Bible was made up of revelatory and non-revelatory Scripture. The revelatory Scripture was without error, while the non-revelatory Scripture contained error or could possibly contain error. Once again we are forced to fall back on reason and human scholarship to try to determine what parts of the Bible are God's revelation and what parts are not. This view also relates to one's interpretation of the concept of revelation and theology. If one defines revelation as the self-disclosure of God revealing to us those things which we would otherwise not know, then one might interpret that there are parts of Scripture that were revealed by God and other parts that were simply common knowledge, part of the historical record or for that matter a part of individual life experience. However, a more acceptable position regarding revelation is that all of the Bible is God's revelation or disclosure to us.

More recently at the Lausanne Conference on Evangelism, efforts were made to draw up a doctrinal position that would satisfy all of the participants. The difficulty was to write a statement regarding the inspiration and the authority of the Scriptures. The compromise position was the "Bible is authoritative in all that it affirms." Even though Francis Schaeffer signed that particular doctrinal statement, shortly afterwards he published a booklet in which he expressed his second thoughts regarding this doctrinal statement because of this very problem. The question that we obviously have to raise is what does the Bible affirm and what does it not affirm. Once again we are forced to fall back on reason and human scholarship for the answer.

Still more recently, as revealed by Harold Lindsell and his book *The Battle for the Bible*, there is a new interpretation of the old statement that the Bible is the "final authority in all matters of faith and practice." The new understanding at least on the part of some, is that faith has to do with initial faith or saving faith and practice has to do only with those things that relate to the Christian life. Things that would fall outside those parameters could possibly be open to question.

Because Christian education is first and foremost a biblical or theological discipline, it must be decided once and for all that the Bible is our final authority and that the Bible in its entirety is authoritative and inerrant. By faith we accept the written record that God has given to us of Himself as absolutely reliable in every detail.

In spite of this controversy, I still believe that the real battle for many of us, as Bible believing Christian educators, is not in the area of the authority of the Scriptures or the place of the Bible in Christian education, but the problem is in the application of the Bible not only in our own personal lives but in the lives of our students.

Second Timothy 3:15 and 16 tells us, "And that from a child thou hast known the Holy Scriptures which are able to make thee wise unto salvation through faith which is in Christ Jesus." Verse 16, "All Scripture is given by inspiration by God, and is profitable for doctrine, for reproof, for correction, for instruction in righteousness." Verse 17, "That the man of God may be perfect, thoroughly furnished unto all good works."

Verse 15 says, "And that from a child thou hast known the Holy Scriptures," and the Holy Scriptures that apparently were able to make Timothy wise unto salvation primarily relate to the Old Testament. But the beginning of verse 16 says "all Scripture," and we believe that this now relates to not only the Old Testament but also to the New Testament. All Scripture has been God breathed. The literal meaning of this word, *God breathed* or *inspired*, is actually *God exhaled* (*theopneustos*). God exhaled and gave to the writers the revelation of all that He wanted to be put down in written form, so that we would have inscripturated the Word of God to us. But Paul says to Timothy that the Scripture that has been God exhaled is profitable first of all for doctrine or for teaching or for instruction. In other words, the Word of God is profitable in terms of the doctrinal content that has been given to us so that we might know the mind of God. Secondly, Paul says that it is profitable for reproof and this is to convict us when we are off the track. If our lives are being judged or evaluated on the basis of the Word of God, then the Word will help to show us when we are not walking in the way of God. Thirdly, Paul says that it is profitable for correction. The Word of God acting as a mirror can help to reveal sin, and then the water of the Word can help to remove the sin and make us clean. In terms of its correcting power, the Word of God has the ability to bring us back onto the track. Fourthly, Paul says that it is profitable for instruction or literally for discipline or for child training. This is the word *paideuo* and is the same word found in Hebrews 12 and translated as chastening. The Word of God has the ability to instruct us or discipline us in the sense that it will help regulate our lives by establishing parameters and then in love discipline us to keep us within the framework that God has established.

The purpose of all of this is to help the man or woman of God to be perfect in the sense that we are outfitted. It must be understood, however, that God's pattern for accomplishing all of this is through obedience to the Word of God.

Once again we are confronted with the problem in relationship to not the place or the authority of the Bible, but the use or the application of the Bible in our own personal lives. In 1 Corinthians 3, the apostle Paul tells the Corinthian believers that he could not speak to them as spiritual, but in fact he had to speak unto them as carnal (fleshly) or as to those who were babes in Christ.

Apparently these believers were not recent converts but they had a low level of receptivity in relationship to the truth of the Word of God. Paul goes on to say that he had fed them with milk and not with meat, because their ability to receive and to act upon the Word of God was at a childlike level rather than at an adult level. The problem here is not that the Bible contains milk truth and meat truth, but that the individuals who are being exposed to the truth of the Word of God are at either the milk level or meat level of understanding and acting upon the Word. Often people will say that John 3:16 is milk truth, while for instance the Book of Ephesians is meat truth, particularly chapters 4-6. The fact is that John 3:16 could be milk truth in the sense that it could provide the insight needed to become a believer in Christ but it also could be a banquet feast for the believer who wants to sit down and spend time studying and gaining all of the richness provided in that one verse. It all depends on the believers level of readiness and receptivity.

Again the problem in 1 Corinthians is not what Paul told them, but their ability to receive and act upon that truth. Actually in 1 Corinthians 11 and 15 we have some rather deep spiritual truth that is given to the believers in this church. Chapter 11 deals with the Lord's table, the communion, and chapter 15 is probably the most outstanding chapter in all of the Bible on the subject of the resurrection.

Apparently the problem of carnality is a problem relating to a lack of experience not knowledge. It usually is a problem for those who have a high knowledge level and a low experience level. In fact in 1 Corinthians 3, Paul says that the problem here was not that they did not know the truth but that they did not properly demonstrate it. Their experience level included the negatives of strife and divisions. He said this was the ultimate proof of the fact that they were walking as carnal believers and not really as mature men.

Hebrews 5:11-14 is another passage that relates to this problem of the use of the Bible in the life of the believer. The writer of Hebrews says that he has "many things to say to them but they are hard to be uttered," and the problem really is that they are "dull in their hearings (plural)." In verse 12 he says that because of the length of time that has actually transpired, they ought to have the capability of being teachers, but they still needed someone to teach them the ABC's all over again. Actually what happened was they became as those who have need of a milk bottle rather than a steak dinner.

Verse 13 says, "for everyone that uses milk is unskillful in the word of righteousness: for he is a babe." Often Bible teachers say that these individuals, because they were unskillful, lacked the ability to "rightly divide the word of truth." That could very well be a part of the situation; however, the word that is translated as unskillful, literally means in the Greek language to "lack experience." The problem with these believers was not the fact that they had not been exposed to the truth, but that they were not experiencing the truth in their daily life. These Christians had the knowledge but lacked the experience in relationship to the knowledge that they had. The writer went on to say in verse 14 that "strong meat (the banquet feast) belongs to those who have become of full age" or literally to the mature individuals, to those who "by reason of use have their senses exercised to discern both good and evil."

Once again let us state very clearly that the problem of carnality or fleshly living as a Christian is to know the truth but to lack experience in relationship to that truth.

One rationalization given by the content-only Bible teacher is that "God has promised that His Word wouldn't return to Him void," referring to Isaiah 55:11. From an exegetical standpoint, it should be noted that this is first of all the word which has gone forth from *God's mouth* that will not return void. Considering the isolated-from-life Bible facts that some teachers attempt to communicate, it is doubtful that the Word of God has ever left the pages of their Bible and entered their own heart or student's heart. From the theological standpoint, the Bible teacher might give consideration to the fact that God's Word has a condemning as well as a redeeming ministry. The truth they are so ineffectively teaching may be able to accomplish God's work only by increasing the responsibility and guilt of the student. Lois LeBar illumines the pedagogical aspect of this passage: Noticing the dozen imperatives in Isaiah 55:1-10, she comments. "This lesson plan doesn't begin with Scripture, but with the pupil. He is first motivated and prepared for the truth . . . The burden of the first half of the chapter is getting people who need the Lord to feel their need. Verse 11 does not promise that under all circumstances the Word will accomplish God's purpose whenever it is spoken."[3]

If the student is truly hungry and thirsty and willing to harken diligently unto the Lord, to incline his ear unto the Lord, to seek the Lord and to call upon Him and forsake his wicked way, then in this setting or in this context Isaiah 55:11 can be applied that the Word "will not return void but it will accomplish whereunto it was sent."

In addition what does the Bible say about its own application?

What is the role of knowledge as presented in this passage? "For this reason also, since the day we heard of it, we have not ceased to pray for you and to ask that you may be filled with the knowledge of His will in all spiritual wisdom and understanding, so that you may *walk* in a manner worthy of the Lord, to *please* Him in all respects, bearing fruit *in every good work* and increasing in the knowledge of God" (Colossians 1:9-10).

Did the apostle Paul just "teach the Word," or did he apply it to people's lives? "And we proclaim Him, *admonishing* every man and teaching every man with all wisdom, that we may present every man complete in Christ" (Colossians 1:28).

What was the goal of Paul's teaching? "Remain on at Ephesus, in order that you may *instruct* certain men not to teach strange doctrines, nor to pay attention to myths and endless genealogies, which give rise to mere speculation rather than furthering the administration of God which is by faith. But the goal of our *instruction* is love from a pure heart and a good conscience and a sincere faith" (Timothy 1:3-5).

Does the Great Commission involve teaching lists or transforming lives? "Go therefore and make disciples of all the nations, baptizing them in the name of the Father and the Son and the Holy Spirit, teaching them *to observe* all that I command . . . " (Matthew 28:19-20).

Even in this key passage, what is the emphasis? Abstract doctrine? Theoretical speculation? Or is it practical value and real life? "All Scripture is inspired by God and *profitable* for teaching, for *reproof*, for *correction*, for *training in righteousness*, that the man of God my be adequately equipped for every good work" (2 Timothy 3:16-17).

## Educational Foundation.

Not only biblical principles, but also teaching principles demand that practical application be included in Bible teaching. Lack of life application causes a lack of relevance, lack of involvement, and less modification or transformation of behavior. Without guidance, the student often cannot see biblical truths as they relate to personal life; therefore they often see no reason to learn them. To understand why there is less involvement, consider this situation: You decide to go on a guided tour, and you pay your money to the tour guide. Before you begin, however, the guide says, "Since I've already made this trip, you won't need to go. I'll just tell you all about it." What would you do? Teachers learn greatly because they are involved. But instead of guiding the pupils through the same type of real life experience, we try to short cut the process by giving them only the product, the end result of our experience. It is *easier* to tell, but less productive than if we take them through the process. On such a guided tour, you would probably demand your money back. Is it any wonder then, why uninvolved students usually consider their time in class a waste?

Someone has said that the difference between philosophers and teachers is that philosophers plant seeds while teachers plant trees. How sad. A final educational reason why clasroom application is necessary is that real learning implies a change of behavior. The ultimate objective in Christian education is character change that is Christ-like. Until ideas and facts are translated into emotion, interest and action (convictions), there is no learning (belief). The student who has merely memorized facts or even concepts is only storing information, while the goal of true learning is the realization or actualization of truth in daily life as demonstrated in true wisdom.

## Suggested Methods of Classroom Application

### Generalization

One common method used in attempting to apply Scripture to life is generalization. There are many variations of this method, but basically the detailed facts of the Scripture are presented, and then a generalization or spiritual principle is extracted; the student may be exhorted to use the principle, or the class may end in a prayer, "Lord bless this truth and apply it to our lives." There are two problem areas in the generalization method: 1) the problem of unguided application, and 2) the problem of moralization.

The basic premise of the generalization method is that if the student knows the truth, he will practice it. This however, is far from what actually happens. There are many barriers which impede unguided application, as pointed out by F. B. Edge. There is the barrier of meaning. "For example, in the Sermon on the Mount, Jesus said 'Blessed are the poor in spirit.' If the student attempted to carry out this injunction of Jesus, what would he start doing next week, specifically, that he has not been doing?"[4] If left on his own, the average student would not make *any* application. The second barrier is that of relationship. The student just may not see the connection between the spiritual truth of the generalization and the particular situation of their own life. Another major barrier untouched by generalization is that of the complex situation. Simple generalizations will seldom meet the needs of the "gray-area" circumstances which complicate our lives. Edge also lists such problem barriers as prejudice and social pressures. In summary, when a student is given a generalization and left to make his own application: 1) he may make a valid application; 2) he may, and probably will, think of all the areas of his life to which he is already applying it, but will neglect the areas where he really needs to apply it; or, 3) he may think of those touchy areas of his life where he needs to apply the truth, and simply rationalize his way out of it.[5]

Moralization is the other major problem of the generalization methods. There often is the tendency to spiritualize or to sound "preachy." Unless care is taken, there is usually little student involvement, and the generalizations are usually not packed with excitement. "Do not pin a moral on your scholar's coat lapel, in the hope that it will of itself soak into his blood and diffuse into his system. . . . A worn and faded precept, from a jaded teacher's mind, has been compared to the dull chill pattering of a November rain."[6] Legalism is an unfortunate outcome of the generalization method. As Christians we hear moral principle after moral principle, until our concept of Christianity is that of lists and rules. Although almost any teaching method may have this danger, special danger exists when the primary means of application is generalization. We must always be concerned with the dynamic doctrinal statement but also the dynamic doctrinal expression in daily life.

### Illustration

Another method which can be used to help apply the Bible to life is illustration. The principle is that the closer you stay to real life the more meaningful your teaching will be. A short, real-life story is told in an attempt to relate the Scriptural truth studied to real life today. In order to be effective, the main point of the story should be the same as the main point of the Scripture lesson. This central point should also be self-evident, pre-eminent and more interesting than any of the incidentals of the illustration. Otherwise, the story may detract from rather than emphasize the main point.

While the illustration method has a definite use, in itself it is insufficient for effective classroom application. First, there is little class involvement; half of the class may not even be listening, let alone thinking. The mind responds to that which makes a strong appeal to the senses. The biggest problem is that of transfer of learning. While the student may see the spiritual truth as it relates to the illustration, the illustration is often not similar enough to his own life experience. Therefore, he still does not see the truth as it relates to his life. "The illustration idea rests on the theory of 'transfer by identical elements.' You verbally create a 'real' situation, as much like an actual experience as possible. The hope is that when the learner finds himself in a similar situation, he'll remember and use the truth taught.[7]

> "A pastor cites as an illustration of failure to 'provide things honest in the sight of all men' unwillingness to honor a commitment. But the illustration doesn't make you think of the vacation you're planning, even though you know it means late payment of some bills. And it doesn't make you think of the paper and pencils you bring home to your children from the office. The principle is the same, the illustration is a good one, *but it is not similar enough to help you relate the truth to yourself.*"[8]

It should be noted that the two methods of generalization and illustration are complementary and can work well together. After bringing out the truth from Scripture, several varied illustrations can be given to show the basic ways it should be applied. Still, this is not likely to touch the nerve of need for all the class. It will not solve the problem just to develop the ability to relate the principle to new situations they will face that week. For truly effective application or life integration, we must look further.

### Case Study - Problem Solving

The case study, or real-life problem solving is similar to an illustration; however, the conclusion of the story is not told. The specific implementation of this often is in role playing. The student is "left hanging" at the climax and is asked "What would you do?" Hopefully as the student thinks through an answer, he will utilize the biblical principle that he just learned in class. "A life situation makes no generalized application, but presents the spiritual problem involved in the lesson in terms of a realistic, specific situation in which the members could easily be involved. It takes the spiritual truth out of the realm of the abstract or theoretical. . . . A conflict is involved; a choice must be made."[9] The confrontation and suspense of the case study and the process of problem solving can be an effective way of getting the minds of the students meaningfully involved. Their interest may also be heightened, because they see the practicality of the theoretical facts. The greater the degree of involvement, the greater the degree of interest, attention and ultimate learning. Well-chosen case studies can discourage "casual oversimplification," i.e., the Bible student (or Christian school student) yawning in class because he has heard it all before, may perk up and realize he does not know it all when confronted by a nitty-gritty problem from life.[10] Sometimes in my own teaching I have presented some rather sticky case studies before beginning to teach a certain subject. Often students naively and unthinkingly choose the "naturally right" course of action, but when they are told their choice is biblically wrong, if they are teachable, they are confronted with their need and whetted in their appetite to find biblical answers.

Here are some basic guidelines in creating and selecting case studies for class use. Make the real life situations sufficiently realistic so that it could happen to one of your students. Obviously, you will not want stories involving hundreds of dollars to tell to small children; change the amount to a figure appropriate for the age group. A case study is more effective when it is exciting; a boring story will not arouse much involvement. Do not make the case study too easy. Generally there are two courses of action possible: the natural course and the Christian perspective. Make sure to include all the temptations and pulls of real life. Do not suggest the alternatives to the class but let them figure them out. You should have some questions ready to prime the pump and prod their thinking. Usually, the case study should be presented in the third person to facilitate an objective attitude.[11]

### Critical Thinking-Questioning Strategies

Questioning can be a vital link between theory and practice in almost any teaching situation. More than a method, a questioning spirit should be the atmosphere of the whole teaching-learning process. But in order to be effective, questions need to aim at more than just memory—they need to thrust the student into the higher levels of thinking, such as interpretation, application and evaluation. (For detailed research into the types and functions of questions, see *Classroom Questions: What Kinds?* by Norris M. Sanders.) Questions that deal primarily with application usually have the following characteristics: 1) They put knowledge to use in a problem-solving way, transferring it to a new situation. 2) They make students deal with whole areas of ideas and skills rather than just with parts. Students must scan the whole field of study to find what principle to apply. 3) The student must rely greatly on his previous learning. Since good application questions give a minimum of direction, he is on his own. "When a student meets a problem in life, there will be no teacher present to give instructions. Application questions give practice in independent use of knowledge."[12]

The following questions are from the seven major categories in the cognitive domain from Bloom's *Taxonomy of Educational Objectives.*

Memory          1. Can the student recall or recognize the basic information involved in the Biblically Integrated Concept (B.I.C.) the Expanded Statement (E.S.), and the related specific content?

Translation     2. Can the student change the basic information involved in the B.I.C., the E.S., and the related specific content into a symbolic form or language other than that in which it was originally learned?

Interpretation  3. Can the student describe relationships existing among facts, generalizations, definitions, values, and skills set forth in the B.I.C., the E.S. and the related specific content?

Application     4. Can the student solve lifelike problems that require the identification of the problem and the selection and use of appropriate generalizations and skills as set forth in the B.I.C., the E.S., and the related specific content?

Analysis        5. Can the student relate or rearrange the material contained in the B.I.C., the E.S., and related specific content into its component parts so that its organizational structure can be understood?

Synthesis       6. Can the student solve a problem using the B.I.C., the E.S., and the related specific content in an original creative manner?

Evaluation      7. Can the student judge the consistency, adequacy, and value of material based on criteria established in the B.I.C., the E.S., and related specific content?

These questions have been restated in order to evaluate the thoroughness of teaching integrated concepts or life application.

The following are two additional models for the higher order of thinking (Critical Thinking) utilizing five levels rather than the often used six or seven levels.

The method of questioning is so big and broad that it deserves a separate study, for there is much more involved in questioning than merely interrogative statements. The case study, for example, is really a form of a question. The student must rely on former knowledge, and with a minimum of direction apply it to a new problem situation.

### Guided Personal Application

No teaching method per se can be considered creative; however, effective application of sound principles of teaching and learning with a variety of teaching methods can assist the teacher to more effectively build truth into the personal lives of individual students. Jesus' approach to ministry was not people oriented but person oriented, and He recognized that the closer you stay to real life, the more meaningful the teaching. He also recognized that the primary role of the teacher was to be a guide, not just a disseminator of information. As a guide the teacher was to stimulate the student to active, meaningful involvement, so that he discovered truth from the process of grappling with truth in a real-life setting. The revelation of God is thus presented in a reality-oriented setting. The result is that the student is brought closer to the point where he can apply the truth to the precise situations in which he is involved. Because

**TEACHER ROLE – Active as teller**

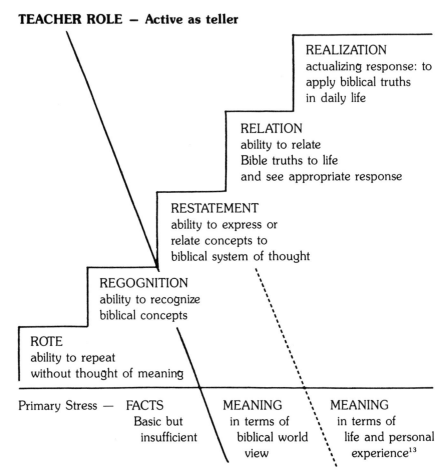

REALIZATION
actualizing response: to
apply biblical truths
in daily life

RELATION
ability to relate
Bible truths to life
and see appropriate response

RESTATEMENT
ability to express or
relate concepts to
biblical system of thought

REGOGNITION
ability to recognize
biblical concepts

ROTE
ability to repeat
without thought of meaning

Primary Stress —    FACTS        MEANING        MEANING
                    Basic but    in terms of    in terms of
                    insufficient biblical world life and personal
                                 view           experience[13]

of personal involvement, interest is heightened and intensified, biblical principles are discovered, the implications are discerned and personal individual student response is encouraged.

Lawrence O. Richards in his approach called Guided Self-Application, divided this process into four basic steps: generalization, varied application, examination of sensitive areas, and personal decision. In *generalization*, the group is led to extract the principle of biblical truth from the lesson. Usually, the students themselves are able to figure out the principle, with the teacher acting as a guide who clarifies or restates and summarizes. Then, the teacher guides the class to see some of the *varied applications* these principles have in real life. Usually a particular aspect of application will appear more obvious and more highly crucial to the students, so the teacher may guide them in a closer *examination of the sensitive area*. This step is a norm, but not a necessity. Finally, the teacher encourages the student to decide on a *specific response* which they will make in their life in light of Scripture.[15]

## LEARNING LEVELS

The Bible can be learned at any of these levels. Creative teaching is teaching to constantly raise students' level of learning toward realization.[14]

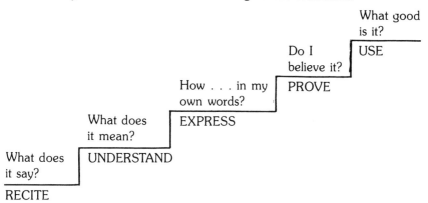

Guided individual personal application can be used in Bible study with any number of methods, from lecture to informal sharing to outside research. Varied application can be centered around a case study but also utilize role-playing situations.

This approach to putting the Bible into a more meaningful real life perspective possesses some promising rewards. Though the teacher cannot be assured that all will participate, the opportunity for enticement will be greater. This whole approach demands the personal involvement of the individual. There is also the opportunity for the exercise of the spiritual gifts of everyone in the class, thus increasing the potential for the class to be a microcosm of the functioning body of Christ. Finally, this approach allows the teacher to resume his proper place primarily not just as a disseminator of information, but as a facilitator of learning actively participating and stimulating learning. There are some potential pitfalls. Such free-flowing discussions about real life can uncover touchy or embarrassing areas in the students' lives. Whether he realizes it or not, each student risks exposing his weaknesses and sins. The things he suggests reveal them.[16] There is also the limitation that this approach requires a group with a great degree of maturity, and its effectiveness can only be realized when the group has been trained in its use. This simply requires that the teacher make haste slowly, being willing to settle for short gains rather than giant leaps.

### Basic Principles

Of the methods discussed, generalization, illustration, case study-problem solving, critical thinking—strategies, question, and guided personal application, all have a place, but they are certainly not the only methods possible. Here are some basic principles to consider in developing a good methodological approach to application.

1. *Not only is personal application essential to Bible study (revelation demands response) but it is also essential to take time in class for application.* Unless time is taken to connect Scripture with life, the connection will probably never be made.

Here are seven "nie niemals" (never, nevers) as we approach our teaching focusing on "character change that is Christ-like."

A. Never teach the Bible purely from an academic perspective. It is possible to know the Word of God from a purely objective standpoint and be able to properly exegete the passages, but we must never lose sight of the fact that the Bible is not just a textbook to be studied. It has been given to us to produce life and to continue to transform our lives into the very image of Jesus Christ.

B. Never teach the Bible without personally applying the truth to yourself. It is possible for the teacher to know the Scripture exegetically and thus to be able to instruct the students on the mental or intellectual plane, but only a teacher who has personally applied the truth to his own life can truly be effective in applying the truth to the lives of his students. Because teaching is basically the impact of life, we must constantly remind ourselves that "the living curriculum" is a vital part of the process of producing life transformation in the lives of our students.

C. Never neglect the personal response of worship (John 4:23; 1 Corinthians 16:22), because "the Father is seeking for those who would be continually worshipping Him." There is the need to express our love and praise and adoration, and this should come as a result of our coming to know more about God, both in terms of who He is as well as what He has done on our behalf. When the Word of God is properly studied, unless the process of biblical abortion takes place, it should cause us to respond in worship to God which should result in our being willing workers in serving Him. First Corinthians 16:22 says, "if any man love (phileo) not the Lord Jesus Christ let him be accursed."

D. Never neglect applying the truth of the Word of God to the lives of your students. As teachers we must continually remind ourselves that we should never take time to teach the Word of God without taking time to apply it to real life. This obviously requires that the teacher have a general background of the characteristics and the needs of the different age groups, their respective lifestyles, as well as their own unique problems. However, in the final analysis, the teacher must get to know his students personally and individually in order to be able to apply truth more meaningfully to individual lives. This requires that the teacher be familiar with home situations, educational background, talents or gifts, unique problems, and any bits of information that would give special insight needed for effective communication. This obviously will take time and sacrifice on the part of the teacher, but will be rewarded with a greater degree of life changing impact.

E. Never neglect reading and meditating personally on the Word of God. Psalm 1:1, 2 says, "How blessed is the man who does not walk in the counsel of the wicked or stand in the path of sinners nor sit in the seat of scoffers! But his delight is in the law of the Lord and in his law he meditates day and night" (N.A.S.B.). The picture of meditating is continually thinking upon the truth and turning it over in your mind so that you are able to extract the maximum benefit from the spiritual food that you have received. It actually is the picture of the cow chewing her cud and then regurgitating the food back into her mouth in order to chew it again and again to extract the greatest benefit from every bite. As Christians we need to fill our minds and our thoughts with the truth of the Word of God so that literally we are "filled with the knowledge of His will in all wisdom and spiritual understanding" (Colossians 1:10).

F. Never neglect assisting others to grow spiritually. Ephesians 5:23 and 1 Corinthians 11:3 suggest to us that as husbands we are ultimately responsible for the spiritual welfare and growth of our wives and our children. First Corinthians 10:24 and Philippians 2:4 emphasize the fact that we should not primarily seek our own good or welfare, but our greatest concern should be for the welfare of others specifically those within the body of Christ.

G. The final "never never" is never forget that it is possible to have a dynamic doctrinal statement without a dynamic demonstration of the truth in the lives of individuals. It is possible to be thoroughly orthodox in our theology but to be thoroughly heterodox in our manner of living. The phenomeneon is that it is impossible to have a truly dynamic demonstration of the truth without having a sound and dynamic doctrinal statement. Yet it is possible to have a propositional Christianity but somehow to miss the personal aspect of Christianity in terms of applying truth to life. John 1:14 talks about the Word becoming flesh, and this obviously applies specifically to the Lord Jesus Christ who took upon Himself the form of human flesh in order that he might "dwell among us." May I suggest that at least in principle what the world desperately needs is for the Word to "become flesh" in each of our lives, so that not only other believers but those in the world around us will not only hear our accurate dynamic doctrinal statement, but they will see the dynamic demonstration of the truth in our lives.

2. *An effective means of directing your teaching toward the practical goal of personal application is to develop the correct type of teaching aim.* If you focus on knowledge—"To know this, to help the students understand this," you probably reach no further goal than that. If your aim is "to help each student identify or distinguish areas in which he may be limiting Christ and to help each begin to trust Him in them," your whole lesson will be structured toward changing lives. Your teaching must aim at response. This implies that you will still be teaching the Bible as information, but information (objective truth) as a means to an end, not an end in itself. It also imples that you understand the Scripture yourself, so as not to be aiming toward some erroneous or inappropriate response.

3. *Correct classroom application is impossible without student participation regardless of the method you use.* You must get your students involved. This invariably will call for a degree of controlled freedom in the group. Class discussion and interaction probably should be the rule rather than the exception. It will demand that the teacher stop being primarily a teller and start functioning as a guide. Of course, even following all the principles, no teacher can be assured that he will communicate to every student. Not even the greatest teacher Jesus, had 100 percent response. But who is responsible for the teaching-learning process? Initially the teacher is 100 percent responsible for the teaching-learning process while the student is 100 percent responsible for the learning-living process. Initially the teacher is 100 percent responsible for the effective communication of the truth (i.e., meaning exchange—and meaning always resides with the hearer not with the sender in the process of communication). Ultimately the student is 100 percent responsible for the effective application or implementation of the truth or the message that is clearly understood. However, in no way can the teacher come away from the Scriptures with the understanding that his only responsibility is to sow the seed or to somehow give out the truth without accepting any responsibility for whetting the student's appetite or of seeking to stimulate the students to imitate or to apply the truth that they have come to know. The startling discovery that one finds in the Scripture is that carnality (sin) is primarily a failure to experience the truth of the Word of God in our personal lives at the same level that we intelligently understand the meaning of the truth.

Apparently one of the primary reasons why Jesus taught truth using parables was to camouflage the truth. In other words, He did not want everyone to be able to understand the truth, for then they would be responsible for it in terms of life application. On the basis of the readiness of the students and their ability to respond to the truth, Jesus explained the meaning of the truth so that now they could see personal application in their own lives. As teachers, our concern should be to guide our students in the process of growing with the Lord so that they may be able to "walk worthy" of (in balance or in equal weight with) the truth that they have come to know.

This is an awesome responsibility. We are not just "teaching the Word," but are aiming at transforming lives. Only two things in the world have eternal value, says Prof. Hendricks, "people and God's Word. And the only activity of lasting value is getting these two together." Like the Master Teacher, today's Bible teacher needs to be a prepared instrument in the hands of the Holy Spirit, weaving the Word into students' hearts and lives.

## Making Bible Teaching More Effective

Life related teaching and especially Bible teaching will tend to be effective:

1. To the extent that the teacher is emphasizing concepts and not just facts. It again must be reinforced that one can teach facts and never teach concepts, but in order to teach concepts the facts must be synthesized into

meaningful relationships. Teaching conceptually is helping the students to get a better handle on the picture, the big idea, and this will enhance the whole integrative or application process.

2. It will be more effective when the Bible teaching is given in an integrative fashion. The teacher must work at not only relating truth with truth but at weaving the truth together with life and ultimately the specific life application to the individual student.

3. Certainly teaching will be much more effective when it is conducted in an atmosphere that is permissive, acceptive, and non-condemning. The student must have the freedom even to be able to expose his own weaknesses and be guided in the process of grappling with the truth in an open non-threatening situation, so that the Spirit of God will have a greater opportunity to apply the truth specifically in his own life.

4. The teaching will be more effective when it is structured according to the problem-solving process. One could teach passages of Scripture or teach truth, but teach it totally unrelated to real life. Teaching on the basis of problem solving forces the teacher not only to teach the passage, but also guide the students in discovering the biblical principles and then continuing further to work through the process of applying those principles to the problems or issues of life.

5. The teaching will be effective in direct proportion as meaningful involvement takes place. Good teaching and learning demands meaningful involvement on the part of both the teacher and pupil as together they interact with the truth and begin applying the truth to real life. The greater the degree of involvement, the greater the degree of interest and thus the greater potential for meaningful learning.

6. The teaching will be much more effective when quality not just quantity becomes the goal. Sometimes in our attempt to emphasize quality we forget the fact that there still must be quantity. The Scripture places the emphasis not on quantity or amount alone, but on the quality of the quantity that is actually given. The example of this is the believer standing before the judgment seat of Christ when he will be judged on the quality of living in relationship to the quantity of truth that he has been exposed to. Again, the reason why Jesus taught with parables was to reduce the potential for judgment, because if the truth were not understood, apparently they would not be held accountable and be judged by it.

7. Teaching will be much more effective to the extent that interpersonal relationships are intensified. The stronger the interpersonal relationships between the teacher and the student, the greater the potential for impact. Our desire is not simply to impact them with information, but to impact them in such a way that there is life change. This requires that teachers be willing to spend time building strong relationships with their students in order that the written Word will make an impact in their life through the modeling of the Word of God in our own lives.

Again we need to be reminded that from God's perspective the acid test is not the way the teacher will normally test the student. Most of the testing of our students is in relationship to the cognitive domain, whereas God is going to evaluate us on the basis of the affective in relationship to the cognitive as well as the behavioral. Here are some specific examples from the Scriptures:

1. In relationship to salvation, it is possible for one to know the truth of how to be saved and yet still be lost. According to 1 John 5:1-5, and 10-13, there is the absolute necessity of placing an active faith in Jesus Christ and thus to experience new life in Christ. It is not just the knowledge alone that makes us a child of God but the experience of that truth in our own lives in relationship to the new birth.

2. The ministry of the Holy Spirit in our own life can be evaluated according to Galatians 5:22-23 on the basis of the fruit of the Spirit. All of these are qualities, traits or characteristics that ought to be evidenced in our lives, and the test is subjective not objective.

3. In relationship to discipleship, John 13:35 says that the test is that we "love one another." Apparently, this is the way that all people are able to evaluate whether or not we are truly followers of the Lord Jesus Christ. The fulfillment of the first and second commandment of Matthew 22:37-39 and Mark 12:30-31 is first of all to love the Lord our God with all our heart, soul, strength, and mind, but the second commandment is to love our neighbor as ourselves. Once again this is not just simply an objective theoretical type of evaluation but is a subjective or practical means of evaluating our commitment to the command of God.

4. Maturity in the life of the believer is also evaluated on the basis of desire for the pure unadulterated milk of the Word of God in order that growth may continue. Ephesians 4:13-16 presents the evidence of a growing maturity in the life of a believer as the fact that we are "no longer tossed to and fro and carried about by every wind of doctrine." But in fact are actually "growing up into Christ" in the sense that we are evidencing character change that is Christ-like.

5. Even the aspect of immaturity as we have already pointed out from Hebrews 5:13 and 1 Corinthians 3:1-3 is the fact that the immature believer is demonstrating this, not because of his lack of knowledge, but because of his lack of experience.

6. The final test of course is the judgment seat of Christ, and in 2 Corinthians 5:10 and 1 Corinthians 3:12-17 the emphasis is clear. The believer is going to be judged or evaluated on the basis of the life he has lived. It is not on the basis of our memorization of Bible verses, our regular attendance at church services or even our faithful giving to the Lord's work that is going to be the acid test. The test is the quality of our living in relationship to the quantity of the truth that we have come to know. Once again it must be clearly reaffirmed that the subjective must always be based on the objective authoritative Word of God. Before there can be personal

experience or expression of the truth in the life of the individual, there must be a solid commitment to the propositional truths that have been revealed to us in God's word.

7. Finally, we must be reminded that on the basis of God's word, the ultimate objective in Christian education is character change that is Christ-like, the demonstration of Biblical wisdom.

1. Lawrence O. Richards, *Creative Bible Teaching* (Chicago: Moody Press, 1971), pp. 56-57.

2. Roy B. Zuck, *Spiritual Power in Your Teaching* (Chicago: Moody Press, 1963), p. 79.

3. LeBar, op. cit., p. 124.

4. Findley B. Edge, *Teaching for Results* (Nashville, TN: Broadman Press, 1956), pp. 130-131.

5. Ibid., p. 135.

6. Theodore E. Schmaud, *How to Teach in Sunday School* (Philadelphia, PA: The United Lutheran Publishing House, 1920), p. 123.

7. Richards, *op. cit.*, p. 118.

8. Ibid., *loc. cit.*

9. Edge, *op. cit.*, p. 140.

10. Leroy Ford, *Using the Case Study in Teaching and Training* (Nashville, TN: Broadman Press, 1969), p. 48.

11. Edge, *op. cit.*, pp. 142-143.

12. Norris M. Sanders, *Classroom Questions: What Kind?* (New York, N.Y.: Harper and Row, 1966), p. 76.

13. Richards, Lawrence O., *Creative Bible Teaching*, p. 75.

14. John Milton Gregory, *The Seven Laws of Teaching* (Grand Rapids, MI: Baker Book House, 1917, 1954), p. 98-101.

15. Richards, p. 121.

CHAPTER 10

# Educational Objectives
# for the Christian School

## Foundational Concepts

It has previously been stated that education is both process and product, impression and expression. When one begins a study of the product aspect of education, it includes a study of the aims or objectives of the process. The problem, however, is that even though on the surface the result or product might appear to be the same, there is little consensus as to the purpose or objective toward which the process was aimed.

Ever since the first adult began to pass on his knowledge to his or to other people's children, there has probably been more or less discussion as to what the training was really for. Such primitive groups as still exist show a diversity in their thinking on this point. A man may teach his son to chip an arrow-head as a technique to be employed at once by the boy in hunting or in self-defense, as a means of preparation for adulthood, as a form of artistic expression, as a training in patience and self-control, as a step in the training for leadership as a means of coming in contact with a divine power, or as training in a trade. The ends would, in these various instances, be utilitarian, preparatory, aesthetic, disciplinary, social, religious or vocational. All of these objectives have existed for centuries, often simultaneously, but the emphasis has usually been on only one or two at once. The main end of education in any single period of history is the one that best reflects the needs of society at the time, but less popular objectives have some followers. In short, mankind has never been able to make up its mind for long about the proper aims of education, and since there are relatively so few of them one finds the same ones cropping up in different centuries whenever the environment is appropriate for each in turn.[1]

Ultimately every educational aim is related to some theory of value. Ways must then be determined in which education can help to achieve or enhance these values.

## Sources of Aims and Objectives

*Individual Needs.* Nothing seems more practical to the average person than the satisfaction of his own individual needs. It is this emphasis on the individual which has led to what is known as pupil-centered or child-centered teaching. Pupil-centered teaching may involve predetermined aims, worked out as best the teacher can from his general knowledge of child life and characteristics, while on the contrary, it may disclaim any preset objectives, letting all aims become contingent upon observed pupil responses.

*Society.* Society has also had a part in determining educational aims. Pointing to the fact that no individual lives in a vacuum, a social orientation of aims would include two factors. First, society has the right to expect the individual to consider the customs and welfare of the group and thus not live in selfish irresponsibility. Second, both in the value of a social setting for education and the satisfaction of the individual needs of wholesome group relationships, society has something to offer the individual.

*Culture.* A cultural education seeks to provide for the individual a knowledge of and appreciation for the best that humanity has acquired and accomplished throughout its history. It attempts to give to the pupil the fruits of civilization. Education that is purely cultural will, of necessity, be largely transmissive rather than creative in methodology. The intellectual and aesthetic areas of life will be dealt with chiefly. Broadly conceived, however, cultural education may include all aspects of life. The education idea of ancient Athens was just that comprehensive. Eby gives the following description:

> Athenian education sought to mold the boy into an intergrated whole through a cultivation of all aspects of his nature. To be a perfect man involved the exercise of all human functions, family life, politics, war, and physical, moral, intellectual, and aesthetic activity. Body and soul, the real and the ideal, individual and public interests, the beautiful and the good, the intellectual and the aesthetic, the rough virtues of the fighter and urban qualities of the gentlemen, were all to be skillfully blended into a single personality.[2]

It can be seen that the Greek ideal of the educated man was one completely developed in all his powers and qualities, thus being "perfect." As such, it is in line with modern efforts to educate the "whole child", though both Greek and modern educators have fallen far short of the desired goal. The cultural aim is not necessarily inconsistent with Christian education, as far as it goes, for it too seeks the development of all of one's capabilities and does so with the help of all who have gone before him.

Sidney Hook outlines a liberal education which, except for the omission of physical training, closely parallels the Greek idea. According to Hook, a liberal education should consist of: (1) knowledge of the physical universe, (2) knowledge of the social environment, (3) knowledge of the nature and consequences of human values and ideals—a philosophy of life, (4) skill in a method of analysis, (5) skill in communication, both oral and written, (6) aesthetics, including discrimination and interpretation rather than mere appreciation.[3] In Hook's analysis the cultural overlaps with other aims such as the social, but the cultural aim predominates.

Most people would readily agree that a sound mind in a sound body is a worthy aim of education, although they might not go so far as to say that it is the end of education.

A domination of the cultural aim may lead to several weaknesses. First, it may exalt human dignity but overlook human sin. The result then may be thoroughly humanistic, ignoring man's spiritual nature and needs. Second, it has even tended to follow the Socratic concept that knowledge is a virtue.

*Religion.* History bears mute testimony to the fact that one of the strongest motives for education has been the religious motive. The first American schools were dominated by a religious purpose that continued to the nineteenth century.

> One learned to read chiefly that one might be able to read the Catechism and the Bible, and to know the will of the Heavenly Father. There was scarely any other purpose in the maintenance of elementary schools. In the grammar schools and the colleges, students were "instructed to consider well the main end of life and studies". . . . Religious matter constituted the only reading matter, outside the instruction in Latin in the grammar schools. The Catechism was taught, and the Bible was read and expounded. Church attendance was required, the grammar-school pupils were obligated to report each week on the Sunday sermon.[4]

Before the American Revolution there appeared a noticeable change of purpose in the schools, from that which was exclusively religious to an interest in preparation for living in this world,

> Due to rude frontier conditions, the decline in force of the old religious-town governments, the diversity of sects, the rise of new trade and civil interests, and the breakdown of old-home connections, the hold on the people of the old religious doctrines was weakened. . . . By 1750 the change in religious thinking in America had become quite marked.[5]

The rise of the academies in competition with the Latin grammar schools is a striking example of this change in atitude. Franklin's academy, begun in Philadelphia in 1751, included modern languages and other practical courses in its curriculum.[6] The Morrill Act of 1862, which brought into being the land-grant colleges, was prompted by a practical and vocational aim.

*Research Commissions.* In 1892 the National Education Association appointed a committee to study public education, with the objective being to secure uniformity of curricula for admission to college and to shorten the period of preparation. Since the committee was chiefly concerned with curriculum, its report made much of the subject matter. Industrial and commercial subjects were omitted in favor of literary and scientific ones. However, with its weaknesses, Eby declares this report to be one of the most important educational documents ever issued in this country.[7]

Though perhaps of even greater significance was the work of the Commission on the Reorganization of Secondary Education, appointed by the National Education Association in 1911. For the first time psychological principles and testing results were employed to determine educational objectives. The results of this committee were the following seven objectives: health, command of the fundamental processes, worthy home membership, vocation, civic education, worthy use of leisure, and ethical character. The importance of the principles lay in the fact that they were an effort

> to show that what secondary education undertook to do should be determined by the needs of the society it was to serve; by the kind of persons who were to be educated; and in the light of available information on educational philosophy and practice. In this report attention was sharply drawn to the rapidly growing complexity of American life and to the relations of the individual to the state and to national and international matter.[8]

In 1944 the Educational Policies Commission of the N.E.A. listed in its *Education for All American Youth* ten results that should be accrued from a good education. The following is a summary of their aims: (1) Develop salable skills for intelligent productive participation. (2) Develop and maintain good health and physical fitness. (3) Understand the rights and duties of democratic citizenship. (4) Understand the significance of the family and conditions needed for successful family life. (5) Understand how to purchase and use goods and services and their economic consequences. (6) Understand the nature of science, its influence, and the main facts of the nature of the world and man. (7) Develop the capacity to appreciate beauty in art, literature, music, and nature. (8) Be able to use leisure time for personal satisfaction and social usefulness. (9) Develop a respect for others and the ability to live and work co-operatively with others. (10) Grow in ability to think rationally, to express thoughts clearly, and to read and listen with understanding.[9]

From the previously mentioned objectives, three observations may be made. While there is an attempt to provide for the entire personality, the obvious omission of any attempt to provide for the individual's spiritual needs leaves it wanting. The one aim which seems to be the focal point for the others is that of social utility. Finally, it is interesting to note that about half of the ten mentioned aims were once responsibilities and functions of the home, only indirectly related to the school.

An additional authoritative statement of aims and objectives is found in the Mid-Century Committee on Outcomes in Elementary Education. This resultant report said that elementary education ought to concern itself with (1) physical development and health, (2) personality development, (3) ethical behavior, (4) social relations within the community, (5) extension of the social world beyond the community, (6) the natural enviornment, (7) aesthetic development, (8) language skills—oral and written, and (9) quantitative relationships.[10]

Here again is an effort to educate the "whole child," but as seen in the previous list of aims the spiritual needs are not even remotely considered.

*Philosophy.* During the last two centuries, two philosophical ideas have caused some educators to refrain from establishing fixed goals. These two influences are subjectivism and relativism. The most important modern expression of the latter is found in pragmatism, which holds that something is true or has worth only if it works in actual experience.

Without danger of controversy, it may be stated that the foremost proponent of pragmatism in education has been John Dewey.

> John Dewey's philosophy is usually called instrumentalism. Instrumentalism -- ideas are instruments of action and their usefulness determines their truth. The implication is that knowledge is not simply a set of facts or a piece of descriptive information. Knowledge and thinking are instruments by which men manipulate the world about them.[11]

John Dewey objected to ultimate goals on the grounds that education is not preparation but the process of living here and now; therefore, remote aims hold no meaning or interest to the child even though immediate aims are acceptable. Thus Edy gains this interpretation of Dewey's thought:

> It is absurd, therefore, to require him (the child) to do things today for the sake of what he will be years from now. The adult is forever trying to make the child act upon ends which only the adult can foresee, but of which the child knows nothing.[12]

For John Dewey there could never be any predetermined or traditional aims or goals. The nearest we could come to saying that Dewey has an objective in view is found in the goal of more activity and more experience. Dewey himself wrote that the "educative process has no end beyond itself; it is its own end."[13] "Ends," in Dewey's mind, ". . . like the acquisition of skills, possession of knowledge, attainment of culture are not ends. They are marks of growth and means to its continuing."[14]

William Heard Kilpatrick, who also is an advocate of a system of flexible or contingent aims or objectives, bases his opinion on the fact of change, which he says reigns in the world. As to ultimate aims and goals, he declares, "To fix absolute standards is to commit us to an impossible regime of denial of adaptation to circumstances."

From the preceding discussion it is seen that with or without fixed or predetermined aims the ultimate goal remains the same, that of educating the whole child. However, even though educators have kept their aims consistent with the ultimate goal, a major area has been overlooked. Because educators believe that they can be neutral in their presentation and that there can be a clean break between the religious (Bible, church) and the secular, the spiritual aspect of man is completely bypassed. This is as it is because ultimately every educational aim will be related to some theory of value and the basic philosophy of secular educators does not allow for aims in this area.

*Specific Objectives for the Christian School*
What should be the educational objectives for the Christian school? The following is the statement of purpose for the Delaware County Christian School in Newtown Square, Pennsylvania.

> In the Delaware County Christian School the seven cardinal goals of education, viz., character, citizenship, vocation, health, fundamental skills, worthy use of leisure, worthy home membership, are fully accepted and set forth through the curriculum. But these goals are enlared by being integrated with an acknowledgment of the triune God and with the revelation of His truth in the Holy Scriptures. The intent is that each student shall have a knowledge of life on the broadest possible plane.
>
> The child thus becomes spiritually fitted for a fruitful relationship to God and is brought into meaningful adjustment personally with today's complex world.[15]

Dr. Roy Lowrie, Headmaster of the Delaware County Christian School for many years, lists in an article in the *Christian Teacher* twenty-two objectives for the Christian school.
1. To teach that the Lord Jesus Christ is the Son of God who came to earth to die for sin.
2. To teach the necessity of being born again through faith in the Lord Jesus Christ.
3. To teach that progress in Christian living depends upon fellowship with God through daily feeding upon the Word, prayer, and service.
4. To teach that each Christian should purpose to yield himself wholeheartedly to God, a sustained sacrifice, obeying all of His will.
5. To teach that a Christian should not, and need not, live his life under the dominion of sin.
6. To teach that the Bible is the only Word of God and is practical and important.
7. To teach that all of life must be related to God if we are to comprehend the true meaning of life.
8. To integrate academic subjects with the Bible.
9. To promote the application of biblical principles to every part of daily life.

10. To show the way a Christian should live in this present evil world.
11. To teach the urgency of world missions.
12. To teach the student to apply himself and to fulfill his responsibilities.
13. To teach the student to work independently and cooperatively.
14. To develop critical thinking.
15. To develop creative skills.
16. To develop effective skills for communication.
17. To teach the knowledge and skills required for occupational competence.
18. To teach Christian social graces.
19. To teach our American heritage and the current problems facing our country and world.
20. To develop an appreciation of the fine arts.
21. To stimulate the desire for wholesome physical and mental recreation.
22. To show the student his present civic responsibilities and to prepare him for adult citizenship with the understanding that government is ordained of God.[16]

The Wheaton Christian Grammar School catalogue contains an effective presentation of well-formulated educational objectives. Not only are their objectives specifically spelled out, but they are listed categorically under the headings of physical, mental, spiritual, social and emotional, all of which can be related to a Christian theistic philosophy of education. The following is a listing of their objectives under each heading:

### Spiritually

"Let the Word of God dwell in you richly."
To lead the child under the guidance and power of the Holy Spirit;
to an experience of being born of the Spirit through personal faith in the Lord Jesus Christ;
into a study and personal application of the Bible so that he will be conformed to the image of Christ Jesus;
to desire to share his spiritual experiences with others.

### Mentally

"Let this mind be in you which was also in Christ Jesus."
To aid in the discovery and development of God-given intellectual abilities and to recognize the Christian obligation to use them constructively;
to stimulate reasoning, academic investigation, creative and critical thinking;
to impart a command of common knowledge and skills and develop ability to adapt in a rapidly changing society;
to develop the individual's mind to its maximum without losing the ability to accept the simplicity of the Scriptures.

### Physically

"Present your bodies a living sacrifice . . . unto God."
To develop coordination, grace, poise in movement, muscle tone and balance, endurance and agility;

worthy use of leisure time.
desirable habits in the care of the body;
a respect for the body as a temple of the Holy Spirit.

*Socially*

"No man liveth unto himself."

To foster respect for parents, courtesy and love for the whole family, and to
    help the child assume, with understanding, responsibility within the family
    unit;

to help the child show his responsibility for good sportsmanship, honesty, and
    concern for the right of others by Christlike involvement in every group to
    which he belongs;

to arouse and promote personal responsibility toward home and foreign
    missions;

to develop an understanding, appreciation, love and respect for all men;

*Emotionally*

"Be strong in the Lord and in the power of His might."

To help the child achieve emotional stability through a personal relationship
    to the Lord Jesus Christ;

develop positive attitudes toward situations and people;

develop sensitivity to the aesthetic;

recognize the Christ-controlled personality as the source of true happiness.[17]

This has not been an attempt to formulate a complete list of educational
objectives, but only to stimulate some much needed thinking in this area. With
the basic foundational concepts clearly in mind, it is now possible to begin to
be definitive concerning specific operationally defined educational objectives
for each specific local situation. Regardless of whether it is from the viewpoint
of the total school program, a specific course, or a specific class hour, there
must be definite predetermined educational objectives toward which the teachers
and school administration can move.

## Reasons for Defining Objectives

The amazing conclusion that can be drawn when evaluating the
accomplishments of a particular organization is that those having specific aims
or objectives in mind can accomplish more. Even apart from this basic and
fundamental reason for having objectives clearly in mind, there are several other
reasons equally as important for defining the educational objectives of a Christian school.

> First, a statement of our objectives clarifies the goals towards which we
> are aiming. Clear perspective gives direction and impetus to our daily work.
> We can make plans for the achievement of objectives. Such planning and
> its execution are right at the core of our program of Christian education.
> Our objectives are the targets to be hit through effective planning.

Second, a statement of our objectives gives us a standard against which we can judge the present status and the rate of progress of our school. How can we evaluate our educational program accurately if we do not have clear objectives to use for our evaluation criteria?

Third, a statement of our objectives is needed for interpreting our Christian school to the public through our public relations program. A printed statement of school objectives can be read and studied by parents who are considering the enrollment of their children in our school. There objectives help answer the question, "What is the Christian school all about?" The explanation of our objectives should be the foundation of our public relations program.[18]

## Summary

It is recognized by educators today that the goal of education is the integration of the personality within a world view. Thus the secular educator attempts the complete development of a personality for complete living. But with the exclusion of God and the Bible the spiritual aspect of man is omitted. That which is to be accomplished is consequently not fulfilled in totality.

Because Christian education does not exclude God and the Bible it is capable of developing the complete personality. Immediately the need arises for a distinctive definition of Christian education. It is a science dealing with the principles and practice of teaching and learning conducted by a Christian teacher for Christians. Both teacher and pupil must be controlled by the Spirit of God and all truth therefore is brought into living relationship with the truth of the Word of God. Thus the whole of the pupil's personality is integrated within a Word-centered Christian theistic world view, for the purpose of enabling him better to serve and glorify God. Because both the teacher and pupil are born again Christians controlled by the Holy Spirit, and the Word both living (Jesus Christ) and written (the Bible) are the integrating forces both in personal life as well as classroom presentation, it can be seen that Christian education is distinctive. Further, a regular Bible course is taught as part of the curriculum and Christian counseling and guidance are available. Finally, in the matter of teacher-pupil and school-home relationships there is a humble attitude as all sit at the feet of the Master Teacher. Parents truly are ultimately responsible before God for their children, but parents and teachers cooperate together for the total development of the child.

The distinctive philosophy of education for the Christian school by choice, not chance, must be a Christian theistic world view. This is presented and elaborated against this background of a word-centered approach. In stating that the educational philosophy is Word-centered, it is believed that the relationship between Jesus Christ, the living Word, and the Bible, the written Word is more clearly shown. Thus, the concept of a God-centered and Bible-centered approach are drawn together in a Word-centered approach.

To give purpose and direction, various sources of aims and objectives in education are presented along with some specific aims and objectives for the

Christian school. Finally, it is seen that the defining of objectives clarifies the goals toward which one is aiming, gives a standard of evaluation for the work being accomplished and helps in the interpretation of the Christian school to the public.

## Conclusion

Education in the Christian school must be distinctive in order to be true Christian education. Secondly, to claim to be a Christian demands a world view based on the Bible. Finally, because secular educators openly deny the existence of God and scoff at the Bible, to be a Christian creates the need for distinctive Christian education. Christian children of today deserve Christian education from kindergarten to university, but today's decisions will determine their destiny.

Some still contend that secular education, though nonsectarian, is still not "godless" as charged because its teachers have learned how to inspire a religious devotion to democratic ideals.[20] Is this Christian education? The ultimate aim of all education for the Christian should be the training of the child to glorify God. "It is the purpose of education to restore man to his God-likeness in the world which God places him."[21]

> Must we be submerged in a secular civilization? Can we afford not to study the world from a Christian perspective? Does not your child deserve a Christian education from kindergarten to university?[22]

The ultimate objective in Christian education is character change that is Christlike, to equip our children to be both functioning members of society as well as functioning members of the Body of Christ.

"Unto the measure of the stature of the fullness of Christ" (Ephesians 4:13-16).

1. Luella Cole, *A History of Education: Socrates to Montesori*, p. 618.

2. Eby, Arrowood and Flinn, Charles, *The History and Philosophy of Education: Ancient and Medieval*, p. 232.

3. Sidney Hook, *Education for Modern Man*, pp. 85-105.

4. Edward P. Cubberley, *The History of Education*, pp. 374-375.

5. Ibid., p. 439.

6. Eby, *op. cit.*, p. 563.

7. Ibid., p. 592.

8. Edgar W. Knight, *Fifty Years of American Education*, p. 105.

9. Ibid., pp. 118-128.

10. Chris A. DeYoung, *Introduction to American Public Education*, pp. 157-159.

11. David Harlin Roper, "The Relationship of John Dewey's Philosophy to Christian Education" (unpublished Master's thesis, Dallas Theological Seminary, Dallas, Texas, 1961), p. 23.

12. Eby, *op. cit.*, p. 619.

13. John Dewey, *Democracy and Education*, p. 59.

14. John Dewey, *Reconstruction in Philosophy*, p. 185.

15. The Delaware County Christian School, *The Delaware County Christian School Manual* (Newton Square, PA: The Delaware County Christian School, n.d.), p. 3.

16. Roy W. Lowrie, Jr., "Christian School Administration," *The Christian Teacher* 110 (May 1960), p. 7.

17. Wheaton Christian Grammar School, *Wheaton Christian Grammar School Catalog* (Wheaton, IL: Wheaton Christian Grammar School, 1980).

18. Statement by Roy W. Lowrie, Jr. in a personal interview, May 1961.

19. Gordon H. Clark, *Christian Philosophy of Education*, p. 192.

20. V. T. Thayer, *Religion in Public Education*, p. 150.

21. Cornelius Jaarsma, *Fundamentals in Christian Education*, pp. 155-156.

22. Clark, *op. cit.*, p. 212.

# CHAPTER 11

# Organizing
# for Curriculum Implementation

## The Importance of Organization

Whenever any group has a common task, organizational structure is necessary. A group that is unorganized can neither determine nor accomplish its goals. In order to survive, this group must have organization, which may be defined in this way: "To arrange or to form into a coherent unity or functioning whole. . . . To arrange by systematic planning united effort."[1] No matter how simple, the organization must contribute at least the following procedures for making decisions and taking action:

1. A procedure for selecting a leader or leaders.
2. A procedure for determining the goals or purposes of the group.
3. A procedure for achieving the goals of the group.[2]

If these goals and purposes are not achieved, the organized group will disintegrate. For this reason, some procedure for evaluating the accomplishment of the determined goals must be developed. Apparently then, the question is: "Does education have a common goal or purpose? Does each individual school have a clear and realistic understanding of its mission?" An institution which does not know its mission, which has not examined all possibilities and focused on a pointed realistic mission, but instead believes it can teach all subjects to all men, cannot expect to survive long. Knowing what the educational goals or purposes are and actually accomplishing them are often miles apart. The first step, then, toward survival is knowing what the school can do and setting out to do it, no more and no less.[3]

Huston Smith in *The Purposes of Higher Education* says, "The most important question any educator can ask is, 'What are we trying to do when we teach?' "[4]

> What is the basic purpose of education? To transmit the past or to control the present? To nurture an elite or to make all men equal? To impart information or to elicit criticism? To cultivate minds alone or men as well? Should it take as its object man universal, stripped of all irrelevancies of time, fortune, and motivational variables of culture and idiosyncrasy?[5]

The answers given today are far from clear. Until the confusion of basic purpose is dispelled by greater clarity and agreement, the possibilities of education will be compromised and only occasionally will the general mediocrity be highlighted by instances of real effectiveness.[6]

To the extent that education is able to specify its goals or purposes, it is the academic calendar organization which provides the structure for curriculum and is a basic determining factor in the development of the entire educational program. Whatever the proposed calendar organization, it should be designed to facilitate the achievement of the aims and objectives of the individual schools. Of the seven basic components of any educational experience, it is the organization structure which relates the experiences provided by the teacher, the student, the curriculum, the facility and the finances which pay for the experience. All of this, however, must be built upon the foundation or underpinnings of the basic educational philosophy.[7]

### The Principles of Organization.

The structural plan of operation in education is not an end in itself. Its only value lies in the effectiveness it contributes to the improvement of the quality of education and the accomplishment of the educational task. Since the teaching-learning relationship is the heart of any educational program, any campaign to improve education should focus on this relationship rather than on the organizational or administrative design.

It must always be kept in mind that organization is a transporting device, a means to an end. Certainly the administrative structure for any organization should be built upon tested principles and caution should be exerted to avoid worshipping any organizational style. Organization is merely the tool or vehicle for accomplishing the goal in an orderly manner. It provides the structure necessary for the accomplishment of the school's purposes and goals. "No organizational plan should be allowed to become so absolute that it cannot adjust to changing demands."[8]

One of the ever present dangers of any curriculum and calendar innovation is that when one school is successful with a new approach, others adopt the new innovations whether or not they may help accomplish their purposes. The problem then is not with the organizational structure, but with the lack of group planning. Organization should grow out of the purposes and needs of the group and be the product of its planning. The parties affected by or involved in carrying out the new organizational policies must be a part of the decision-making process. Group planning will help the individual members to function within the organizational structure.[9]

Organization should be flexible rather than inviolable. An inflexible organization can stifle the quality of creativity. Provisions should be made to keep the organizational structure flexible in order to be responsive to unanticipated needs. The administrative organization should be flexible so that a variety of learning activities may be carried on both in and out of the classroom. In an autocracy, where all orders are handed down from the top, there is little group planning and involvement. This becomes a natural breeding ground for discontent and lack of cooperation.[10]

Organization should provide for maximum participation on the part of the group in the decision-making process. This is especially true where groups are directly affected by or are involved in carrying out new policies.[11]

Organization should be integrated. Coordination and integration of functions, activities, interests, and assignments are necessary for the successful accomplishment of the purpose of the institution. Every unit should be coordinated to the objectives of the whole. Consent is an indication of affirmative acceptance of the new policy but integration, ideally, is better because it takes into account that those who are to implement the proposal have from the outset been a part of its formulation and adoption.[12]

Rather than putting the lid on creativity, proper organization stimulates individual creativity and through an increase in the ideation process develops innovative programs. Organizational structure should produce, not stifle, creativity related to the personnel and program under consideration.[13]

Educators must always be concerned with organization and organizational patterns, but they must constantly be on guard lest concern for innovation in curriculum and calendar organization obscure the reason for which all else exists, the student, the teaching-learning educational task.

## Patterns of Curriculum

In an attempt to achieve desired goals, man has endeavored to organize his environment. Several times educators have organized and reorganized the calendar year in education in an effort to facilitate better teaching and learning. However, no one calendar organization seems to excel over all others, though several patterns have emerged. The following material regarding higher education illustrates the point.

If the total number of weeks that a student spends on campus during his undergraduate studies is approximately 120, (15 weeks x 8 semesters) then these weeks could physically be divided a number of ways. During the early history of higher education in the United States, the academic year was almost exclusively divided into two semesters of 14-17 weeks. This organizational plan seemed to be more manageable and also reserved the summer months for students to return to an agrarian society or to seek other types of employment conducive to the warmer months. In this way students are able to provide financially for their next year of study.[14] The semester plan still is the preferred calendar pattern though there is no reason it has to be *the* calendar structure of higher education.

In the 1930s and 1940s some state and private institutions developed a "quarter system" of approximately ten weeks each. Under this system the period from September to June has three study periods. The fourth quarter or study period takes place during the summer. While many institutions continue to operate on this calendar plan, most schools have only three quarters and for a few the added summer quarter is used primarily for "catch up and not go ahead" work.[15]

After World War II, the tri-mester (tri-semester) calendar pattern was adopted by some schools.[16] Those who promoted this plan indicated that by offering courses all year, campus facilities and faculties could be better utilized as well as allow the student to complete his college requirements in three years. However, organization of facilities and personnel for year-round service proved to be costly and periods of time for needed renovation of buildings and equipment were not available. Also it became apparent that few students wanted to remain under rigorous study conditions for that extended period of time. Many needed time to recoup financially. Though the tri-mester was accepted in theory, it died just as suddenly as it became popular because the social mores of our country could not be changed.[17]

In theory, the typical undergraduate program of approximately 120 weeks could be:

1. One term of 120 weeks
2. Two terms of 60 weeks
3. Three terms of 40 weeks
4. Four terms of 30 weeks
5. Five terms of 24 weeks
6. Six terms of 20 weeks
7. Seven terms of approximately 17 weeks
8. Eight terms of 15 weeks (often called the "semester")
9. Nine terms of 13.3 weeks
10. Ten terms of 12 weeks
11. Eleven terms of almost 11 weeks
12. Twelve terms of 10 weeks (often called the "quarter")[18]

Calendar organization or reorganization can be delineated by months. Some of the patterns in operation are:

1. 6-6 Antioch College (work-study program)
2. 4-1-4 Eckard College
3. 4-4-1 Wortburg College
4. 4-2-4-2 Centre College
5. 4-1-4-1-2 Mars Hill College

6. 4-0-4 Kansas University
7. 3-3-1 Hanover College[19]
8. 4-4-2-2 Brigham Young University
9. 2-2-1-2-2 Ottawa University
10. 4-1-4-1-1 Tarkio College

Calendar Organization or reorganization can also be by weeks:

1. 10-3-10-10 Mercyhurst College
2. 10-4-10-10 Maryville College (Tenn.)
3. 12-12-6 Elmira College
4. 13-13-6 Wellesley College
5. 12-8-12 (3-2-3) Furman University[20]

There is one thing common to all of these programs. Each has attempted to adopt changes to fit specific needs existing on the individual campus. As colleges introduce curricular change, it is believed there will be increasing modification of the college calendar.[21]

For further study of the subject of curriculum and calendar innovation see author's doctoral dissertation: A Discriptive Study of the Historical Development of 4-1-4 Calendar Organization and Its Related Administrative and Curricular—Instructional Innovation," University of Missouri-Kansas City, 1974.

## Conclusions

The following five conclusions are apparent regarding curricular and calendar innovation.

1. *Curricular and calendar innovation is dependent upon the school's philosophy as interpreted through the administration.*

The schools that apparently have thought through and brought into focus their philosophy of education, by involving themselves in a rather complete evaluation of the curriculum and total program, were the schools that have been able to do the most with the calendar organization innovation of 4-1-4, (Fall semester -- one month Interterm [January] -- Spring semester). Apparently without the adequate philosophical underpinnings to support the program for curriculum changes, the calendar organization change from a quarter system or a semester system to 4-1-4 was ineffective in and of itself. In one of the schools involved in the study, the faculty seemed ready for the curricular calendar innovation, but the administration apparently was only paying lip service to the proposed innovation. Possibly because schools are facing dropping enrollment, the administration (because of their awareness of the financial difficulties of the institution) was grasping for something that would inject new life into the institution and hopefully to curtail if not stop the attrition rate as well as potentially rejuvenate the recruitment program. However, even with an adequate philosophy that the administration first and foremost is thoroughly committed to, there is no adequate delineation of the program the school is desirous of implementing. As a result schools are literally groping in the dark for the type of calendar organizational structure that will best facilitate their purposes. Also change generally is accomplished by ultimately getting to the source of control. With the administrator sitting in the driver's seat, change or innovation must move from the top down. The interesting phenomenon is that in at least one school there was a serious commitment on the part of the administration, yet they apparently were never able to communicate this adequately to the faculty members. Even though the idea for rethinking philosophy and implementation of curricular calendar innovation started from the top, this concern never was able to filter through the entire ranks of the institution.

2. *Administrative efforts must actively support and contribute to curricular and calendar innovation.*

Once again in relationship to curricular and calendar innovation, in each of the schools where administrators saw themselves as part of the supportive team doing all they could to contribute actively to the change or innovation, 4-1-4 and any related curricular-instructional innovation was potentially more successful. The schools that were able to provide administrative and secretarial personnel to handle the increased work load caused by another entry point into the school's program were able to prevent or at least reduce the possible conflict between the administration and faculty members. Also the provision of support personnel greatly facilitated the ease with which the students were able to enroll in Interterm, and therefore became an encouraging rather than a discouraging factor. Finally, the schools where the administration saw the contributory effects of Interterm to the total instructional-learning situation rather than an opportunity to collect more tuition and fees from the students, are the schools where the curricular and calendar innovation of 4-1-4 seems to be much more successful.

3. *Faculty members must be willing to address themselves to the issues of curricular and calendar innovation.*

Where the schools engaged in considerable long range planning and total faculty involvement in thinking through the issues of curricular and calendar innovation, these schools have been able to move more smoothly into 4-1-4 and the related curricular-instructional innovation and are experiencing more success. Apart from the commitment of faculty members to the necessity of thinking through the issues as well as a total commitment to an educational philosophy that demanded innovation or change, as soon as the 4-1-4 innovation was implemented and the problems became a reality, faculty support quickly waned. The schools that have been the most successful in implementing 4-1-4 are the ones where faculty members were willing to think through the issues of curricular and calender innovation. Because of faculty commitment to an educational philosophy that focused not only on teaching but also upon learning, no matter what issues or problems became apparent they did not become a deterrent to discourage or sidetrack them from commitment to the necessity of curricular-instructional innovation.

4. *Administration and faculty must be committed to creativity and regard innovation as a surmountable challenge.*

Once again schools where the educational philosophy created a commitment to discovering new ways to make learning more meaningful were the ones where innovation was not something nice, but absolutely necessary and therefore a challenge to be surmounted. When administrators and faculty members were able to work creatively in a team effort, the entire school became committed and therefore each problem and issue simply provided another challenge to be overcome. To the extent that the faculty and administration saw the necessity for creating new and more meaningful learning situations for the students, commitment to innovation and change was considered a necessity rather than thinking that creativity and innovation were things that simply caused more work without really making any improvements.

5. *The dimensions of the normal learning experiences must be enlarged and adapted to the conditions of Interterm.*

Even though a school did not make a major curriculum overhaul in the winged semesters, if the courses provided during Interterm were simply regular catalog courses taught in the usual manner, the heightening of faculty interest to become committed and involved was extremely remote. This was also true of motivating students to commit themselves to this intense experience. Without the availability of independent study opportunities as well as on and off-campus learning experiences and a variety of other available options, Interterm is essentially doomed before it gets off the ground. It seems that the greater the flexibility and the availability of options to design innovative courses and programs during Interterm, the greater the potential success of this program. The intenseness of a three or four-week experience, not only for the faculty members but also for the students, requires an increased flexibility. Care must be taken to design courses that will provide a meaningful teaching-learning experience, without killing the motivation of both the faculty members and students, and so exhausting them both that they are really ineffective as they begin the second semester. If the January Interterm is simply one course from the regular semester compressed into a four-week block of time and taught in the traditional lecture, teacher-centered approach, there is little chance that students will be sufficiently motivated to desire involvement in the Interterm program each year.

Once a school is (1) thoroughly committed to a philosophy that demands curricular and calendar innovation, and (2) the administration is able to adequately interpret this to the faculty and is willing to support and contribute actively to the innovation, and (3) faculty members are willing to address themselves to the issues of curricular and calendar innovation, and (4) both the administration and faculty are committed to the necessity of innovation and see it as a surmountable challenge, and (5) are willing to provide a structure and format which allows more flexibility for designing courses and programs, to this extent it seems that a school has reason to expect success in the implementation of curricular and calender innovation.

**Recommendations**

*Criteria for Selecting Calendar Organization*

What are the criteria for selecting calendar organizational structure? The following is a recommended ten-point criteria to be used in selecting and evaluating calendar organization.

1. The calendar organization should reduce the fragmentation of the learning experience and result in less stress.

Any proposed academic calendar should be particularly designed to reduce the fragmentation of the student experience and reduce the extraneous nonproductive stress resulting from the demand of the schedule of taking four to six courses simultaneously. Assignments, examinations, and paper deadlines, when taking a larger number of courses, clearly determines how a student spends his study time. The reduction in the number of courses should minimize the stress resulting from the feeling of living from one crisis to another.

2. The calendar organization should provide a natural setting for intensive student-faculty contact.

The concentrated effort upon fewer courses, especially the one course for the Interterm should provide greater opportunities for closer contact between students and faculty. This certainly is important for the achievement of the primary educational objectives of any institution.

3. The calendar structure should provide maximum flexibility for the educational program.

Because of individual differences in students, some emphasis should be placed on the desirability of a flexible educational program. Certainly planning of the student's program should be done on a yearly basis, however, a more flexible calendar organizational structure would provide for additional opportunities for the student to alter his plan during his educational career.

At the same time, the instructor should have opportunity for greater flexibility in structuring courses. Since students may be taking fewer courses, it conceivably could be easier to arrange the schedule of course meetings in accordance with the desires of the instructor and the limitations of the classroom situation. Thus, the limitation of an inflexible time slot for each class period could be eliminated.

The calendar structure should also provide greater flexibility in developing additional independent study opportunities for students. It should be relatively easy to set up such courses as these become important to the student's educational progress and fit into his program. It is also possible that advanced students could spend all or a least a major portion of one of their terms in independent study. Likewise, it would also be possible for students to be involved in their academic program throughout their calendar year if they wish to accelerate their program toward completing the course of study.

More flexibility should also be provided for other aspects of in-depth study such as study away from campus, field trips, or community study and more in-depth research.

4. The calendar should provide opportunities for off-campus experiences at times when it is desirable in the student's program.

The restlessness of today's student population is in part due to the role of the observer which the educational process demands of students. The opportunity for participation would help channel these energies into constructive activities and aid personal development. The possibility of a shorter time block would permit the scheduling of such experiences at times when the student is in need of them without disturbing the development of his educational plan.

Off-campus experiences provide opportunities for a number of desirable experiences as well as for introducing more unity into the life of students who seek to relate their intellectual activity to the world around them. Shorter time blocks in the calendar would also allow sufficient flexibility for a student to take time off from his studies or to include in his program an off-campus experience so as to enhance rather than disturb the development of his educational program. The short period of time in which a student either works with professionals in his chosen vocation, or participates in on-going programs in which the student has interests, could very well allow him to better plan his programs and future developments.

5. The calendar organization should optimize the amount of time in which the student is engaged in the learning process.

The greater concentration of a given subject coupled with the concentration of faculty attention to fewer groups of students and subject matter would: (1) Permit a reduction of the number of formal examination periods as the student would view the subject matter *in toto*; (2) allow the faculty member to evaluate progress through his daily contact with the student.

A reduction in the number of formal evaluation periods would tend to reduce the stress generated by the constant necessity to prepare for examinations. A more relaxed approach on the part of a student to a learning experience would make him more aware of values which have been emphasized traditionally in a course: namely the intrinsic value of the subject matter, the methodology, and the structure of the knowledge under study.

6. The calendar should be structured to allow for an improved sequential organization.

The student and his advisors should be able to arrange the course sequence to facilitate the learning experience by taking advantage of courses which complement each other. This would be possible because the student would be enrolled in fewer courses at any given time.

7. The calendar should be structured to facilitate greater efficiency in the learning process and free additional time for educational and other activities outside the classroom setting.

The intensive study promoted by the 4-1-4 or modular calendar will reduce retroactive and pro-active inhibition (interference of one subject with another in the learning process) and can lead to better retention. Thus, less time should be spent relearning concepts which have been forgotten due to lapses of time and attention to too many other subjects. Increased learning efficiency may free time for the student to participate more fully in academic activities outside the classroom or to enjoy the pursuit of his own non-academic interests.

Also, the possibility of having fewer class meetings of longer duration than the traditional fifty minute period could also result in more efficient use of class time.

8. The calendar should allow for a more manageable faculty load.

Two key variables determine a faculty member's work load. The number of separate preparations he has to make during the week and the number of students with whom he comes in contact during the week. The 4-1-4 or modular calendar would reduce the preparation time by concentrating the faculty effort on fewer subjects. The increased concentration of effort resulting from fewer course preparations at a time should also lead to greater efficiency for faculty members who would prepare larger blocks of material at a time and waste less time in the "warm up" phenomenon as he shifts from course to course.

The reduction of load generated by fewer preparations, the possibility of greater efficiency and the redistribution of student load due to basic changes in general education should have the combined effect of allowing the faculty member more time during each semester and during each year for reading, research, work with students, etc.

9. The calendar structure should allow the faculty members large time blocks for research, participation in refresher courses, writing and other scholarly pursuits.

Each faculty member would be expected to teach on the undergraduate level approximately seven courses per year. How these courses are spread out could be arranged in different ways.

10. The structure of the calendar should facilitate more economical operation of the educational program.

The proposed calendar organization should facilitate an expansion to a year-round operation. The 4-1-4 or modular calendar organization can easily be adapted to year-round operation by simply adding three consecutive one-month blocks for the summer school sessions.

In summary, it appears that in applying this ten-point criteria for calendar organizational selection that the 4-1-4 or other modifications of this modular scheduling approach would allow students added flexibility in planning their programs, an opportunity for more productive academic work with greater involvement in the subject matter and less stress. It would also allow faculty members more time for class preparations, research and contact with students, and it would provide a better situation for involving the entire academic program, particularly off-campus experiences and independent study periods. It would also enable certain economic advantages to be gained in the educational program.

1. *Webster's Seventh New Collegiate Dictionary*, 1963, p. 594.

2. Edgar L. Morphet, Roe L. John, and Theodore L. Reller, *Educational Administrations, Concepts, Practices and Issues* (Englewood Cliffs, NJ: Prentice-Hall, Inc., 1959), p. 54.

3. Richard L. Meeth, "Innovation in Liberal Arts College Admission" (Unpublished speech, September, 1969), p. 1.

4. Smith, *op. cit.*, p. 1.

5. Ibid.

6. Ibid., p. 2.

7. Richard L. Meeth, "Seven Faces of Developmental Curricula" (unpublished paper, January 25, 1970), p. 1. (Mimeographed.)

8. Robert E. Wilson, *Educational Administration* (Columbus, OH: Charles E. Merrill, 1966), p. 93.

9. Ordway Tead. *The Art of Administration* (New York, NY: McGraw Hill Book Company, Inc., 1951), pp. 183-184.

10. Wilson, *op. cit.*, pp. 529, 538.

11. Tead, *op. cit.*, p. 183.

12. Wilson, *op. cit.*, p. 95.

13. Ibid., p. 93.

14. Roger Morris Holmes. "Influences of the 4-1-4 Plan on Curriculum and Administration" (unpublished Ed.D. dissertation, Indiana University, 1972), pp. 2-3.

15. Meeth, "The Organization of Higher Education."

16. Holmes, *op. cit.*, p. 3.

17. Meeth, "The Organization of Higher Education."

18. Jack L. Armstrong, *An Interim Term Digest*, revised ed. (St. Paul, MN: Macalester College, 1971), p. 15.

19. Ibid., p. 15.

20. Ibid., p. 16.

21. Michael Brick and Earl J. McGrath. *Innovation in Liberal Arts Colleges* (New York, NY: Teachers College Press, Columbia University, 1969), p. 126.

# CHAPTER 12

# Pluralism Pro and Con

Pluralism can have both a strengthening as well as potentially weakening and even devastating effect. The New Testament uses the figure of the organic church, the body of Christ. Through the ministry of the Holy Spirit, believers are brought together into the "one body." Not only are these individuals from a pluralistic background educationally, socially, racially, culturally, but even theologically. Yet when bonded by the ministry of the Holy Spirit, this pluralism can provide strength and have a positive effect rather than being in and of itself destructive. In addition, the Scripture is clear on the fact that each believer (Ephesians 4:7) has not only been given grace but a sufficient proportion of grace according to the measure of the gift or gifts that God has sovereignly bestowed. From passages such as 1 Corinthians 12 and Romans 12 it is apparent that not every believer has the same gift. Even though within the body of Christ there is diversity, a pluralism of spiritual gifts within the context of diversity or multiplicity in the body of Christ, the Holy Spirit provides the unifying factor to temper or strengthen the diversity and bring the pluralistic elements together into a powerful force rather than causing them to self destruct.

As I began to explore the areas of pluralism within the church-related school as well as in the broad spectrum of the Christian day school movement, I discovered that there were a great many areas where one could identify pluralistic elements. In fact I began to conclude that there were actually more specific elements of pluralism as opposed to singularity or a common agreement in terms of specifics. Pluralism will be examined in five specific areas of the Christian school. We will focus our attention on the teacher, students, the curriculum, finances, and finally the area of philosophy which relates also to theological questions. Each of these five loci will be examined not only in terms of the specific elements of the Christian school that relate to it, but also by using the elements of pluralism, including the theological, educational, the social, cultural, and the academic. Then we will attempt to discover the unifying factors that provide the strength necessary to weld the pluralistic elements of the church-related and independent Christian school into a positive force for the cause of Jesus Christ and His Church.

There are many approaches to teacher preparation and teacher certification. They run the gamut from only requiring that the teacher be a born-again Christian (Accelerated Christian Education) to the requirement that teachers be fully certified in the grade level or in the subject area where they will be teaching. Some forty states (e.g., New York and Indiana) do not require certification of teachers for private schools but in some cases the Christian schools in these areas may require certification along with the additional work required for teaching in a Christian school. Even state certification requirements vary from state to state. In states such as California, teacher certification with the Association of Christian Schools International is sufficient to fulfill the requirements for teaching in a Christian school.

Programs for the preparation of the teachers also vary from the traditional teacher education program found at the state university to the teacher education programs in Christian liberal arts colleges, which are in some cases almost identical with those of the university. Not even when the school has a Christian emphasis is there a guarantee that a course in history and philosophy of education will enable a prospective teacher to develop a consistent and coherent Christian philosophy of education for teaching within the framework of the Christian school. Young people who have graduated from the Christian liberal arts college are sometimes sent into the public school as a mission field with a wide open door. Even though the door is open it is not wide open and one is not welcome in the public school espousing particular Christian convictions and a Christian world and life view.

For a long time it was felt that the only place where teachers could be adequately prepared for the Christian Day School was in the Christian liberal arts college, but among the Christian school leadership there is now more of a movement in the direction of the Bible college. Though it is recognized that often the Bible colleges are not able to prepare teachers beyond the elementary level or possibly eighth grade because they lack the content or subject area for secondary certification, they can quite adequately add the additional courses necessary to prepare the perspective teacher at the elementary level. One of the disadvantages of the Bible college programs is that though they are recognized by the state they do not provide the teacher certification necessary in many of the Christian schools today. In some cases the lack of certification is because the colleges themselves lack regional accreditation. In some cases it is because the Bible colleges insist that if they call their courses education courses (Ed.) rather than Christian education (C.E.) and if these courses have descriptions that are essentially the same as the course descriptions found in the state university catalog then they lose their distinctiveness in being able to prepare Christian teachers. From experience, in the state of Missouri it was discovered that course titles, course descriptions, and course numbering could be modified to satisfy state requirements even though specific course descriptions, course objectives, and actual content were handled from a uniquely Christian education perspective.

Even though more and more of the Christian schools are requiring college graduates and teachers credentials, along with normal requirements of being a born-again believer and other specifics relating to the individual's personal Christian life, the certification may come from a variety of sources and in some cases only be that the Christian School considers the teacher qualified, not certified. Today, however, most Christian schools are looking for truly born-again believers who are not only certified but qualified both to work with children at a specific grade level and in a specific subject area.

What are the reasons for students attending Christian schools? It is interesting to discover that the largest single professional group in the United States sending their children to the Christian school are public school teachers and administrators. This might give us some clue as to some of the reasons why parents are sending their children to the Christian school today. Many parents are concerned about lowered academic standards and lack of discipline in public schools. These may or may not be problems but with the media focusing so much attention on the rampant misbehavior and rising crime and violence in the public schools, to the point of actually declaring them to be a battlefield, many parents are frightened and are looking for legitimate alternatives. For Christian parents, the Christian school becomes one of the strongest and most feasible alternatives. In regard to lowered academic standards, they fear a disregard for academic excellence and an inability to achieve academic excellence.

An interesting comparison is with the early days of the Sunday school movement in this country. In the early 1800s, the Sunday school in the United States was forced to develop as a para-church organization outside the context of the local church. There were many pastors in the early days who opposed Sunday school, insisting that parents would bring their children to the Sunday school expecting the Sunday school to fulfill the responsibilities that God had given to parents directly. Unfortunately, there was an element of truth in that prediction that is once again surfacing as a serious problem in the Christian school. In my conversations with many Christian school administrators across America today, the unanimous conclusion is that the strength of the Christian school is in direct proportion to the Christian home or homes that are represented in the school family. Unfortunately there are many Christian parents who send their children to the Christian school not to complement or supplement what is going on at the home and church but, for all practical purposes, to attempt to fill the void or vacuum.

Ten years ago Christian schools were not as acceptable socially as they have suddenly become today. Parents who would not have considered sending their children in the 1960s or early 1970s have discovered, within the social context of the evangelical church, that the Christian school is not only educationally but socially a status symbol. In some cases because of the rise in tuition costs parents on the lower end of the economic spectrum have been forced to remove their children from the Christian school while only those who are financially able can continue to send their children at a fee of $1,500-$3,000 per child. Little or no tuition aid money is available.

Another interesting phenomenon is that though Christian parents may be reasonably supportive of Christian schools at the elementary (K-6) level, many become extremely supportive at approximately the junior high level. Unfortunately, their young people have often developed such poor discipline patterns and study habits (and a variety of problems of which they are sometimes not even aware) that when they come into the Christian school they may do more to pull the Christian school down rather than help it to continue to be uniquely a *Christian* school. Careless recruitment for the Christian school can, in four to six years at the junior high and senior high level, totally change the character of the school.

Probably in the context of the private school, or more specifically the church-related school, the problem of discipline can be best dealt with. But there is no consistency as to the specific approach even though there is argument that discipline and classroom control are necessary prerequisites for learning. Dress codes are still a controversial area. Some schools not only have specific conduct standards for students while they are at school, but some regulations that also apply off campus. These are obviously difficult if not totally impossible to enforce, but there are many Christian schools that feel that if a particular standard has been established it should be adhered to not only during the hours school is in session but as long as the student is enrolled in that institution. There is no commonality of agreement regarding the specific approach in this area.

A final matter relating to students deals with the social or cultural background of the individual students attending the Christian school. The typical student attending the Christian school is from white, middle class, suburbia. This is not so much by design but more by necessity, particularly from the financial standpoint. Few, if any, of the Christian schools have available monies for student aid and the various minority ethnic groups and inner city families lack the needed financial resources to underwrite the expense of the Christian school. There are probably few Christian schools capable of meeting government standards regarding the enrollment of minority groups in their student body. This is not necessarily a criticism against the Christian schools *per se*, but is certainly a cause for concern among the evangelical churches that have not accepted their responsibility for providing the privilege of a Christian school education for all Christian young people from kindergarten through the college level regardless of race or ethnic background.

The third area that demonstrates pluralism in the Christian school is curriculum. In relationship to textbooks in the Christian school, no one publishing house stands out as the primary supplier for Christian schools. In most subject areas there are Christian schools still using the secular or public school textbooks available. Though many of them are gradually changing to the Christian school textbook suppliers, the lack of quality materials that are uniquely intergrated from a Christian perspective causes many to continue to look to the secular sources. Christian schools use textbooks from Christian school suppliers such as Bob Jones University Press; A-Beka Books, Pensacola, Florida; Accelerated Christian Education, Lewisville, Texas; and Alpha-Omega Publications, Tempe, Arizona.

The Christian school has never widely and universally adopted any one particular Bible curriculum for use in all of the Christian schools. Materials go all the way from adapted Sunday School materials to those specifically designed for use on a day-to-day basis in the Christian school classroom. Here are just a few of the ways that the Bible curriculum is developed in the Christian school. A number of schools are using prepared curriculums such as those available from Bob Jones University Press, as well as the Lifeway curriculum originally produced in California and now produced and distributed by Scripture Press Publications in Wheaton, Illinois. Child Evangelism materials are used with minor adaptation, especially in schools that have as one of their primary emphases evangelism or soul-winning among the students. In some cases even Sunday School materials are being used, though in these cases from publishers different from those being used in the regular Sunday Schools of their own churches. If one interdenominational publishing house is used on a Sunday basis, then another like Roper Press materials might be used in the Christian school.

One of the greatest problems that has always faced the Christian school is the subject of intergration, or the relationship of truth with truth and ultimately the relating of this intergrated truth meaningfully to the life of the student. Very few of the textbooks and Christian materials presently available have really come to grips with this problem, and this is the heart of the problem of the Christian school. In order truly to have a Christian school, we must have teachers for whom the truth of God's Word has been woven into their lives as well as into the subject area that they are going to be teaching. Then the teacher, becoming a part of the living curriculum, is better able to take the printed materials and the teacher-student interaction and bring that truth meaningfully into relationship to the life of the student. In most cases the textbook materials are simply secular textbooks that have been dry-cleaned or made acceptable from a Christian perspective. The approach usually is to eliminate words, phrases, or illustrations that might be unacceptable to the various groups using the materials. In some cases even the pictures or illustrations are changed because of the particular dress styles that create a problem. However, even removing all of the objectionable things and adding Bible verses and scriptural thoughts here and there does not make it truly a Christian book. True integration in Christian education is relating concepts from the discipline with the biblical concepts and ultimately weaving them together into a single, larger, expanded concept. If it is true that all truth is God's truth, then truth in essence is not inherently in conflict with the revealed truth of the Word of God. Most of the materials today do not deal with integration but at best only correlation.

In the financial area we see a variety of approaches. While almost all of the schools require tuition there is no uniformity as to the amount. The differential may be anywhere from $500 to $1,000 per year up to $3,000 or more per school year per student. In a few cases schools have even attempted to operate strictly on the basis of faith and though they have made suggestions to the parents as to the amount of money needed to educate the children, it has been strictly on a freewill basis. It is rare for schools to exist in this fashion for very long. Vitally tied to the matter of tuition are teacher salaries. Higher salaries require higher tuition. Though there is still a long way to go in regard to salaries, Christian schools have made considerable progress in the last decade. In 1970 Christian schools were paying 50-75 percent of the salaries that the same teacher could make in the public school whereas at the beginning of the 1980s salaries have risen to between 75-90 percent of public school salaries. Still starting salaries range from $15-20,000 per year for first year teachers and $20-25,000 for beginning adminstrators.

Few if any of the Christian schools accept any direct state aid or government money, though some are accepting this aid indirectly, in the form of busing, transportation, special education programs (such as driver's education or various remedial programs that may be required by the state but would not be available in the Christian school apart from some financial assistance.) The whole problem of government aid also spills over into the area of tax credit or the voucher. Though there is no clear decision on this matter, it is possible that within the next decade there will be some relief for parents, utilizing either tax credit on income tax or direct financial assistance in the form of a voucher. Though most schools would be willing to allow parents to utilize the tax credit, there are some schools that have already determined they will not accept the voucher money, sincerely believing that if they do so they will immediately subject themselves to additional standards imposed by the state or federal government.

In 1968 when I was taking a survey to discover what the basic problems were in the Christian school movement, from the list of sixty-eight different problems it became quite apparent that the chief problem in Christian schools was lack of finances to be able to do adequately what they believed God had called them to do. Though the size and shape of the problem has changed in the last twenty or twenty-five years, it has in no way diminished and perhaps has become more acute. But the ways of raising money, charging tuition, paying teachers salaries, accepting government aid, and the like, are as varied as they can be.

Pluralism also appears in the Christian school in relation to philosophy of education. As I was preparing for the writing of my master's thesis on the subject of "The Philosophy and Educational Objectives of Christian Day School" and looked at the list of sixty-eight problems that I received from Christian school leaders all over the United States and Canada, I discovered that after removing all of the problems related specifically to finances the remaining problems had as their underlying theme a lack of understanding as to why the individuals were involved in doing what they were doing. The underlying problem, other than finances, was an inadequate philosophy. A philosophy of education should provide the direction for the Christian school in the accomplishment of its specific objectives. However, when one looks at the reasons why Christian schools have been brought into existence, it is obvious that there are a variety of reasons. Back in the 1950s and 1960s, in many cases Christian schools were brought into being for negative reasons. There were problems in the public schools and as a result pastors and Christian parents became concerned about starting alternative schools to provide the proper Christian influence for their children. Many of these schools became so strong in their negative emphasis that they became known far more for what they were against than what they were for. This in some cases had an adverse effect upon some Christian parents who felt this was not a proper environment to produce a positive educational impact. A well-known educator from this century has said that anything that has started for negative reasons seldom ever has any positive results.

More recently Christian schools have been brought into being because of problems relating to crime and violence and lowering of academic standards, but this is not a sufficient rationale for starting a Christian school. The underlying problem relating to the public school is not program or personnel, but the fact that the public school system has been built upon a philosophy of complete and total neutrality. From the Christian perspective this is totally unacceptable, for any education that leaves God out is an education that is unacceptable for us as Christians. Thus for the education of our children at the elementary and secondary level, God, as He has shown Himself to us in His divine revelation, the Bible, must be at the very center or core of our curriculum. Everything that is taught and done must be brought into rightful and meaningful relationship with God and His Word.

In addition to the basic philosophical questions, there are also the related areas of accreditation, licensing, and state requirements. At the present time in the state of Michigan there are over seventy Christian schools that would be classified as operating illegally. What this means is that for a variety of reasons these schools have chosen not to seek licensing by the state, even though in some cases they may be able to meet all the requirements established by the state. What these schools particularly are saying is that because the church sees the Christian school as another vital arm in its educational ministry, the state has no right to tell them what to do or how to operate their schools. Unfortunately, in some cases, the attitude that seems to be projected is that as Christians involved in Christian education they are almost "above the law." However, in some cases it is a sincere and honest attempt to protect the children from the control of Caesar. These schools and parents believe that parents alone are the ones who are ultimately responsible, and therefore the government or the state has no right to dictate in these areas.

In relationship to the philosophy of education, what about the denominational background or sponsorship of Christian schools? There is no one particular denominational group that seems to have an edge on Christian schools, though for a church or group of individuals to have a commitment strong enough to be involved in the development and support of a Christian day school there has to be a strict adherence to the authority of God's Word. Without a strong adherence to the doctrine of the Word of God being verbally inspired and authoritative and inerrant, most groups would not have a strong interest and concern for becoming involved in the Christian school ministry.

After going though so many different areas where there seems to be little or no agreement or unanimity, I began to raise the question in my own mind, "What in the world is holding this school system together?" I do believe that there are some unifying threads that help to tie the pluralism or the diversity within the Christian school into a unified whole. Even though there is not unanimity in most of the areas relating to the Christian school, there is a true unity that binds not only the individual school but the majority of schools together into "God's school system" for this age.

The first unifying factor is a belief in a sovereign God. Because we recognize that God is one and God is sovereign, regardless of what is happening in our culture and in our world, we believe that God is still on the throne and that His commands, His principles, still are true today.

The second factor is a complete and total adherence to the inspired, infallible, and inerrant Word of God. Recognizing that God is sovereign and that His Word is authoritative, the approach of the Christian school requires that God and His Word be at the center of everything we do. Though secular educators may talk about integration, they are never able to come to a common agreement as to what the unifying factor may be. In Christian education we are not searching for the unifying factor, for it is found in the person of God Himself as He has revealed Himself to us through the written Word as well as the Living Word, the Lord Jesus Christ.

A third unifying factor is personal dedication and commitment to the person of Jesus Christ as well as to the accomplishment of the cause of Jesus Christ as delineated in the Great Commission. There is a growing commitment to the fact that one of the greatest means for discipling our boys and girls and young people today is to bind together the church, the school and the home into the total package of building into these young people the truths that they need to know, but also providing them an opportunity to learn how to apply or live these principles meaningfully in their daily lives. With teachers and adminstrators who are dedicated first of all to implementing these things in their own personal life but also in the lives of students, there is a greater potential for being able to produce results in the lives of the students that demonstrate this high level of dedication and commitment.

A fourth unifying factor is academic and spiritual excellence. It is difficult to be able to maintain a high level of academic excellence and still be able to maintain a high level of spiritual commitment, not only in terms of our doctrinal position but also in terms of our daily practice.

It is generally agreed among Christian school leaders that the ultimate objective in Christian school education is to equip our young people not only to be functioning members of society but also to be functioning members of the body of Christ. The ultimate objective of Christian school education is character change that is Christ-like (Ephesians 4:11-16—Unto the measure of the stature of the fullness of Christ). The fifth and final unifying factor, then, is that Christian school education is the means to the end of developing young people who demonstrate character change that is Christ-like. Thus more and more Christian schools are looking for teachers who can become a part of the living curriculum within the school. They are also looking for curriculum materials that will assist the teachers and the students alike in growing in grace and in the knowledge of the Lord, not only growing in the knowledge of the Lord Jesus Christ but in their ability to be living, clear, observable models of the reality of Jesus Christ in the contemporary world.

Pluralism in the Christian school? Yes! Unanimity in the Christian school? No! Unity within the Christian school? Yes!

**Chapter 13**

# Developing Excellence
# in Christian Education

Where do we go from here? It seems to me that excellence in Christian education must ultimately be achieved by developing Christian educators who strive for excellence in personal growth, practical growth, and professional growth.

## Personal Growth

The first item of concern in the area of personal growth is that the Christian educator must be filled (controlled) with the Word of God. These are desperate days of conflict in relationship to the authority and inerrancy of the Word of God, and Christian educators need to clearly declare themselves in relationship to the centrality of the Word of God. Almost more than being known as educators, Christian educators today must be known as men and women of the Book. Second Timothy 2:15 does not primarily emphasize the command to "study" as much as it emphasizes what our attitude toward the Word of God should be. The verse says that we should "Be eager to show ourselves approved unto God, workmen who need not to be ashamed, rightly dividing the word of Truth." Certainly our eagerness to be approved demands not only a thorough study of the Word of God, but as good workmen we must approach the Word of God using good methods. The end result is that we will not be ashamed as we are able to rightly handle the Word of God.

Secondly, the Christian educator must be filled (controlled) with the Spirit. Ephesians 5:18 is clear when it states, "Be not drunk with wine, but be continually filled or controlled by the Holy Spirit." The apostle Paul is saying that we should not be drunk with wine in the sense that we never even allow it to get started; but in striking contrast we should be allowing the Holy Spirit to continually fill or control our lives.

It is true that in most instances when the Scripture mentions being filled with the Holy Spirit, the emphasis immediately following is on something related to verbal ccommunication. However, there were demonstrations of action, things the individual(s) did that occurred either before, during, or after the speaking but always in relationship to being filled with the Holy Spirit. Actually the fruit of the Spirit is love, and this *agape* love could involve verbal expression, but it demands action. *Agape* love involves the will, is not motivated by "what can I get" but "what can I give," and is willing to give and give even though it knows it will receive nothing in return. All of the other eight qualities (joy, peace, longsuffering, kindness, goodness, faithfulness, meekness [strength under control], self-control) could as well be demonstrated in a person's manner of speech, but would best be shown in the manner of living, the actions of the individual.

Part of our problem in understanding the concept of the *filling of the Holy Spirit* is that Paul in Ephesians 5:18 uses the analogy of being drunk. He does not say, however, "stop being drunk," the kind of Greek construction he uses in Ephesians 4:30—"stop grieving the Holy Spirit"—or in 1 Thessalonians 5:19—"stop quenching the Holy Spirit." What he is saying is: "Be not drunk with wine in the sense that you never even let this thing get started." I am only using this as an illustration and in no way am I somehow endorsing drinking or drunkenness. But what does the analogy mean?

Dr. Daniel Noonan, a medical doctor from the University of Illinois, in discussing alcohol and drug use states that the thing that happens to persons in the first level of intoxication is that they lose their inhibitions. He illustrates by explaining that a salesman who is uptight could be helped while a pilot who has to make precise, split-second judgments would be hindered through alcohol use. However, we must hasten to add that the medical doctor warns that a person could become dependent on alcohol and without realizing it become an alcoholic. I think the general agreement would be that a person's speech is one of the first things affected when they lose their inhibitions.[1]

Thus, when a person is controlled by the Holy Spirit, he also loses his inhibitions; but rather than the results being negative, the works of the flesh, they are positive, the fruit of the Spirit. Apparently Paul is telling us that as believers in the Body of Christ, we need to lose our inhibitions, become untied, loosed, set free by the power of the Holy Spirit.

The last thing that happens to a person when he is totally drunk is that he loses his integrative ability. Dr. Noonan explains it this way. The person who is normally a very moral, ethical, upright individual, now because he is totally drunk, loses his ability to make a transfer of his attitudes, values and standards from one area to another.[2] I believe that the person who is controlled by the Holy Spirit is the individual with the greatest potential for integration. This obviously is not some automatic process but apparently the potential is available.

What we desperately need in Christian education are teachers who because of the ministry of the Holy Spirit have lost their inhibitions and are able to develop warm, friendly, caring personal relationships with students and have gained the greatest spiritual enablement to integrate truth with truth and ultimately truth with life.

Regardless of whether you translate the Greek preposition in Ephesians 5:18 or Galatians 5:16 as "in" (in the sphere of) or "by" (by means of an enablement the Holy Spirit), the fact remains that it must be the work or ministry of the Holy Spirit.

Recently I was watching someone buy some tropical fish. The clerk took the fish from the tank and put them in a plastic bag filled with water. She then blew into the sack and tied it shut. The question then is, what difference does it make whether the fish swims around in the bag (in—locative—sphere) or if he lies at the bottom of the sack (by—instrumental—by means of)? The important thing is only that the fish must be in the plastic bag. The important thing is that every believer has all the Holy Spirit (Romans 8:9; Galatians 4:6—Holy Spirit **5** Spirit of Christ) all of the time from the moment of conversion (1 Corinthians 6:19—temple **5** holiest of holies).

Some believe that because the "filling of the Holy Spirit" relates to speech and not actions, you cannot connect Ephesians 5:18 with Galatians 5:16. Though I agree that speaking is probably the first area affected when a person is drunk either with alcohol or with the Holy Spirit, the context of the passages relating to "filling" are not limited to speaking.

Ephesians 5:18-21 is really all one sentence, and following the "filling" of verse 18 there is the "speaking" in verse 19 and "giving thanks" in verse 20. However, in verse 21 there is an action described—we are to "submit" ourselves to one another. More specifically the verses that follow beginning at verse 22 and going at least to 6:4 give to us the roles and relationships of family members.

Another example of this is Saul (Acts 9:17). In verse 17 he is "filled," verse 18 he receives his sight and is baptized, and in verse 19 he eats and is strengthened, remaining with the disciples. Finally, also in verse 19, he proclaims Christ in the synagogues. I definitely believe that the filling of the Holy Spirit not only affects my speech, but my whole manner of living. Galatians 5:16 states then that we should walk, taking each and every step by faith, by means of the Holy Spirit; then we will not fulfill the lusts of the flesh. The apostle Paul in 1 Corinthians 2:15 has made it very clear that the spiritual person—that is, the individual who is filled or controlled by the Holy Spirit—has the ability to examine or differentiate all things. This is specifically in relationship to the Word of God, but I believe it also applies to "all truth."

Finally, in the area of personal growth the Christian educator must be balanced. Ephesians 4:1 says that the believer is to walk worthy or worthily of the calling. The Greek word for *worthily* is the picture of a balance beam, and apparently Paul is using it to indicate that a worthy walk is a walk that is in equal weight with or in balance with what the individual knows regarding the truth of the Word of God.

It is significant to note that the apostle Paul makes reference to the word *walk* only twice in the first three chapters of the Book of Ephesians. The first time is in reference to the former walk of the believer (2:2), while the second is in reference to the future walk of the believer (2:10). Apparently Paul's emphasis in chapters 1-3 is first of all on the believer's position, seated with Christ in the heavenlies, and then he emphasizes that the believer needs to learn to stand in this position in Christ. It is only after the believer has learned how to stand that Paul then emphasizes the believer's walk, but it is to be a walk that is in balance with what the person knows regarding his exalted position seated with Christ in the heavenlies.

J. M. Price, the great Southern Baptist educator, says in his book *Jesus the Teacher*, "Jesus lived the truth more than He was able to teach it."[3] The problem of course for us is that we can teach the truth far more than we are able to live it. The danger that must always be guarded against is that our knowledge level must not greatly exceed our ability to experience the Word of God that we have come to know. As the believer stands before the judgment seat of Christ, the apostle Paul tells us in 2 Corinthians 5:10, we are going to be judged on the basis of what sort of life we are living, but always in relationship to the truth from the Word of God that we know. The judgment apparently is on the quality of life in relationship to the quantity of truth from the Word of God which we have come to know and understand.

**Practical Growth**

Certainly every Christian educator recognizes that the laboratory for our ministry is our home (where we live). It is relatively easy to teach the truth of God's Word in a classroom situation, but the real test comes in whether or not we are able to live the truth of the Word of God before the other members of our family in our home. Without a doubt, the home is where the heart is revealed. In the pressure cooker situation of family life, the real you will always surface, and you find yourself completely exposed and bare as you stand before your loved ones in your family. Dr. Henry Brandt often publicly says that "circumstances don't make you, they reveal you," and this certainly would be true of the family situation in the home.

Whatever a Christian educator does, he must come to grips with the fact that his home is not essential to his ministry; it *is* his ministry. I believe that for all practical purposes, to fail in the choice privilege and responsibility that God has given us to minister to our families in our home is to fail in the ministry of top priority that God has given us. Every command of Scripture that relates to the nurturing or training of children has been given to parents, and often specifically to fathers. And now abides the church, the school and the home, these three, but the greatest of these is the home.

## Professional Growth

The apostle Paul has given to every Christian educator a behavioral objective that is worth striving for. Philippians 3:13, 14 says, "Brethren, I count not myself to have apprehended (to have laid hold of): but this one thing I do, forgetting those things which are behind, and reaching forth to those which are before. I press toward the mark for the prize of the high calling of God: in Christ Jesus." Certainly every Christian educator needs to be pressing toward the mark of improving or upgrading his professional competency.

Let's take the word *press* and use it as an acrostic for five suggestions for improving our professional growth. First of all, *professional organization.* Certainly every Christian educator ought to give serious consideration to the professional organization that specifically relates to his or her field. This is an excellent means of keeping abreast of what is happening in the field as well as providing interaction with other professionals.

The second area is *reading.* This, of course, is not only reading in the area directly related to your particular field, but also in related areas that will sharpen your abilities as a professional educator and keep you on the cutting edge of what is happening in your field.

Thirdly, *educational advancement.* Certainly there are seminars and possibly even summer school or extension classes available from Christian colleges, seminaries, the university or community college that can provide educational opportunity. Again this would not only be in relationship to an advanced degree, which certainly will be invaluable, but also to provide you with the fresh update in relationship to the field of Christian education.

Fourthly, *seminars and conferences.* There are many of these that are being held today, such as the National Institute for Christian School Teachers and Administrators, and it would be well for every Christian educator to participate in at least one professional growth seminar annually. It is easy to find yourself constantly giving out without taking the time to be professionally filled or updated yourself; so these seminars can be invaluable.

The fifth and final area is simply personal *study.* This obviously requires a great deal of discipline, but regardless of what it takes it must be done. This would not only be study in relationship to educational concepts, but often Christian educators, even though they do not neglect a more devotional study of the Word of God, often fail to take the time to really study and come to grips with the truth of the Word of God not only for their own lives personally, but also for their discipline or professional ministry.

First Corinthians 15:58 gives us a final summary of the kind of suggestion that I have been trying to put forth. "Therefore, my beloved brethren (in the ministry of Christian education), be ye stedfast, unmovable, always abounding in the work of the Lord (in Christian education), knowing that your labor (in the glorious ministry of Christian education) is not vain or empty."

So what! Where do we go from here? Christian educators must continue to strive for personal, practical and professional growth in order to fulfill the principle given to us by the apostle Paul in 2 Timothy 2:2—"And the things that thou hast heard of me among many witnesses, the same commit thou to faithful men (men who are full of faith), who shall be able (competent) to teach others also." Are you personally striving for competency as a Christian educator? I believe on the basis of the Word of God that this is something that is not optional, but absolutely imperative.

1. Dr. Daniel Noonan, "Drug Interactions With Alcohol," cassette, series 400-6, 1972.
2. Ibid.
3. Price, *Jesus the Teacher*, p.2.

# Bibliography

*A Guide for Curriculum in Christian Education.* New York: Division of Christian Education, National Council of Churches, 1955.

Association for Supervision and Curriculum Development. *Balance in the Curriculum.* Washington, D.C.: The Association, 1961. Examines in detail the attributes which must be evident if the school curriculum is comprehensive and complete.

Benjamin, Harold. *Saber-Tooth Curriculum.* New York: McGraw-Hill Book Co., 1939. Short saterical treatment of curriculum.

Blamires, Harry S. *The Christian Mind: How Should a Christian Think?* Ann Arbor, MI: Servant Books, 1978.

Bloom, Benjamin S. (ed.). *Taxonomy of Educational Objectives, Handbook I; Cognitive Domain.* New York: Longmans Green and Co., 1956.

Bruner, Jerome S. *The Process of Education.* Cambridge: Harvard University Press, 1960.

Bushnell, Horace. *Christian Nurture.* Grand Rapids: Baker, 1979.

Byrne, Herbert W. *A Christian Approach to Education.* Milford, MI: Mott Media, 1977.

Cantor, Nathaniel. *The Teaching-Learning Process.* New York: Dryden Press, 1953.

Chadwick, Ronald P. *Teaching and Learning: An Integrated Approach to Christian Education.* Old Tappan, NJ: Fleming H. Revell, 1982.

Chapman, William E. *Roots of Character Education.* Schenactady, NY: Character Research Press, 1977.

Cully, Iris V. *The Dynamics of Christian Education.* Philadelphia: Westminster Press, 1958.

Dewey, John. *The Child and the Curriculum: The School and Society.* Chicago: University of Chicago Press, 1956. Explains Dewey's philosophy of education.

Edge, Findley B. *Teaching for Results.* Nashville: Broadman Press, 1956.

Eavey, C. B. *Principles of Teaching for Christian Teaching.* Grand Rapids, MI: Zondervan Publishing House.

Ford, Leroy. *Using the Case Study in Teaching and Training.* Nashville, TN: Broadman Press, 1969.

Gaebelein, Frank E. *The Pattern of God's Truth.* Chicago: Moody Press, 1968.

Getz, Gene. *Sharpening the Focus of the Church.* Chicago: Moody Press, 1974.

Jaarsma, Cornelius. *Fundamentals in Christian Education.* Grand Rapids: Wm. B. Eerdmans Publishing Co., 1953.

Krathwohl, David and others. *Taxonomy of Educational Objectives. Handbook II: Affective Domain.* New York: David McKay Co., 1964.

Kraybull, Donald B. *Mennonite Education.* Pennsylvania: Herald Press, 1978.

LeBar, Lois E. *Education That Is Christian.* Old Tappen, NJ: Fleming H. Revell Co., revised 1981.

Mager, Rogert F. *Preparing Instructional Objectives.* Palo Alto: Fearson Publishers, 1962.

May, Philip R. *Which Way to Educate?* Chicago: Moody Press, 1975.

Michaelis, John, et. al. *New Design for the Elementary School Curriculum.* Boston: Allyn and Bacon, 1967.

Miller, Randolph Crump. *Education for Christian Living.* Englewood Cliffs, NJ: Prentice-Hall, Inc., 1956.

Ozmon, Howard and Sam Craver. *Philosophical Foundations of Education.* Columbus: Charles E. Merrill Publishing Co., 1976.

Popham, W. James and Eva L. Baker. *Planning an Instructional Sequence.* Englewood Cliffs, NJ: Prentice-Hall, Inc., 1972.

_____.*Systematic Instruction.* Englewood Cliffs, NJ: Prentice-Hall, Inc., 1970.

_____. *Establishing Instructional Goals.* Englewood Cliffs, NJ: Prentice-Hall Inc., 1970.

Rian, Edwin H. *Christianity and American Education.* San Antonio, TX: Naylor Co., 1949.

Richards, Lawrence O. *A Theology of Christian Education.* Grand Rapids: Zondervan, 1975.

_____. *Creative Bible Teaching.* Chicago: Moody Press, 1971.

Rushdoony, Rousas. *Intellectual Schizophrenia.* Presbyterian and Reformed Publishing Co.

Sanders, Norris M. *Classroom Questions: What Kinds?* New York: Harper & Row, 1966.

Sisemore, John T. (ed). *The Ministry of Religious Education.* Nashville: Broadman Press, 1978.

Stein, Robert N. *The Method and Message of Jesus' Teaching.* Philadelphia: West minister Press, 1978.

Taylor, Marvin J. (ed.). *Religious Education: A Comprehensive Survey.* New York: Abingdon Press, 1960.

Tyler, Ralph W. *Basic Principles of Curriculum and Instruction.* Chicago: University of Chicago Press, 1950.

_____. "New Dimensions in Curriculum Development." *Phi Delta Kappan*, 34, (September, 1966), pp. 25-28. Volume 24.

Vieth, Paul H. (ed.). *The Church and Christian Education*. St. Louis: Bethany Press, 1947.

Watson, Goodwin. *What Psychology Can We Trust?* New York: Bureau of Publication, Columbia University, 1961.

Westerhoff, John H., III. *McGuffey and His Readers: Peity, Morality, and Education in 18th Century America*. Nashville: Abingdon Press, 1978.

Wyckoff, D. Campbell. *Theory and Design in Christian Education Curriculum*. Philadelphia: Westminster Press, 1961.

Zuck, Roy B. *The Holy Spirit in Your Teaching*. Wheaton, IL: Scripture Press Publications, Inc., 1963.